AI BUSINESS STRATEGIES

Leveraging Artificial Intelligence as a Competitive Advantage

BOB PELLERIN

CTOBOB

ISBN-13 Hardcover Edition: 9798390411940
ISBN-13 Paperback Edition: 9798393464110

2nd Edition (August 2023)

Cover concept and design by: Bobby Pellerin

Printed in the United States of America

To Todd Johnson, Ric harris and Kenneth C. Grainger
for their friendship and unwavering support.

FOREWORD

As the CEO of Vocodia.com, I have been privileged to witness firsthand the incredible power of AI in driving growth, innovation, and profitability for businesses of all sizes and across a wide range of industries. However, I know that for many companies outside of the IT sector, the prospect of leveraging AI can seem daunting and overwhelming.

That's why I am excited to introduce you to Bob Pellerin's best selling book "AI Strategy: Leveraging Artificial Intelligence as a Competitive Advantage". This book is an invaluable resource for any business leader who is interested in exploring the possibilities of AI to drive growth and increase profitability.

Bob provides practical, accessible advice and real-world examples of companies that have successfully implemented AI to achieve significant revenue growth. He breaks down complex concepts into easy-to-understand language, making it accessible even for those without a technical background. I can attest that Bob played an instrumental role in the development from the early stages of our AI solution called DISA, which has revolutionized the industry and continues to be a driving force behind our success.

Whether you're in manufacturing, retail, healthcare, or any other industry, "Using AI to Increase Profits" offers actionable insights and strategies for leveraging AI to transform your business. From optimizing supply chain management to improving customer experience, the potential applications of AI are virtually limitless.

I highly recommend this book to any business leader who is interested in staying ahead of the curve and thrive in today's dynamic business environment. It is a must-read for anyone not wishing to get left behind by their competitors.

Brian Podolak
CEO & AI Innovator
Vocodia.com

INTRODUCTION

My introduction to Artificial Intelligence (AI) came in the early 2000s after my tenure at Microsoft and MiconPC. I worked for Montana State University as a technology transfer specialist. My mandate was to review leading edge technology and find applications that solved corporate challenges. These were some technologies that were declassified by the military.

I was given access to the experts and their patents. The aim was to give American corporations and industries a competitive edge by making use of a lot of research that might otherwise fall by the wayside. As you can imagine, searching for a use for some of these projects was challenging. I made a career of thinking outside the box, so using my imagination and sometimes unusual approach worked well in this sort of environment.

I came across an AI system developed at substantial cost. I saw a tangential application for this technology in the financial industry, and so I selected it as a development candidate. Working closely with Montana State University, we were able to prove that the AI modeling system could provide improved statistics. It turned out that AI, when provided with enough data, could predict human behavior. This was a game changer for that industry.

I went on to apply AI to other industries with favorable results over the next decade. The core technology evolved. The programming languages changed. The ways to apply AI changed. Systems got faster. Memory and storage increased dramatically. Networks became faster and more reliable. Alternate processors arrived on the market. GPUs (Graphical Processing Units) provided a huge processing advantage in some cases.

These combined enhancements allowed AI systems to learn exponentially faster. They could now process more data, look at more potential future states, and even help to design future AI systems. This led to better results, applicable to more specific and daunting challenges.

AI is rapidly transforming industries, from healthcare to finance, from manufacturing to retail. As technology continues to evolve, more and more organizations are recognizing the potential for AI to provide a competitive advantage. I have since worked on AI specific services and products, such as helping Vocodia.com elaborate the concept and surmounting challenges from the onset. I am also working to bring AI to those with limited technological skills, such as the elderly. I am convinced AI can be a force for good.

Implementing AI successfully requires more than just investing in technology. It requires a well-crafted AI strategy that aligns with an organization's goals, culture, and capabilities. In this book, we explore the key components of an effective AI strategy, including identifying use cases, building a data infrastructure, developing talent, and managing ethical considerations. We provide practical guidance on how to develop and execute an AI strategy that can drive business value and enable organizations to stay ahead of the competition. Whether you are a business leader, technology executive, or AI practitioner, this book will provide you with the insights and tools you need to leverage AI as a competitive advantage.

As with so many aspects, remember to get input from all stakeholders, from the CEO to the people that produce your wares and services. While some will perceive AI as much needed innovation, others may see it as a step towards eliminating their jobs and ruining human prosperity. What AI does for you, for your environment, for your future is entirely in your hands.

Bob "CTOBOB" Pellerin

Contents

"Artificial intelligence is the new electricity. It has the potential to transform everything we do, but we have to figure out how to harness it effectively first."

Andrew Ng, Co-founder of Google Brain and Coursera.

CHAPTER 1

The Growing Importance of
AI in the Business World

In recent years, artificial intelligence (AI) has emerged as a transformative technology that is changing the way businesses operate. AI has the potential to provide companies with a competitive advantage by improving efficiency, increasing accuracy, and unlocking new insights. As a result, AI has become a top priority for businesses across all industries. Chances are you are already using AI as it is integrated into your browser, your office applications and a variety of cloud services.

One of the key drivers of the growing importance of AI in the business world is the explosion of available data. Big data, data warehousing, and the Internet of Things (IoT) have caused the amount of data being generated by businesses to grow exponentially in recent years, and traditional methods of processing and analyzing this data are no longer sufficient. AI offers a solution to this problem by providing the ability to process large amounts of data quickly and accurately. We call this process '**ingestion**', and it's a term you'll hear quite a bit in the context of exposing an AI to new data.

Another factor driving the importance of AI is the rise of digital transformation. As companies seek to become more agile and responsive to changing market conditions, particularly in the wake of a world shaking pandemic that crippled so many traditional brick and mortar businesses, they are turning to technology to help them offer an online portfolio of goods and services. AI is a key component of this digital transformation, as it enables companies to calculate the best way to automate processes, improves their decision making as to which product and service transformations will be profitable, and creates new business models.

AI is also becoming increasingly accessible to businesses of all sizes. As the technology has matured, the cost of implementing AI solutions has decreased, making it more affordable for smaller companies to take advantage of the benefits of AI. In addition, there is a growing ecosystem of AI tools and platforms that make it easier for companies to implement AI in their operations. As of 2023, some of the very best AI frameworks are open-source, so the barrier to entry is mainly expertise and Cloud computing time.

The benefits of AI for businesses are numerous. For example, AI can be used to improve customer service by providing personalized recommendations and putting customers in priority support queues if it determines they need emergency help. It can also be used to automate routine tasks intelligently, freeing up employees to focus on higher-value activities. In addition, AI can help companies identify patterns and trends in their data that may not be apparent to human analysts, enabling them to make better decisions.

Despite the growing importance of AI in the business world, there are some challenges that must be addressed. One of the biggest challenges is the shortage of skilled AI professionals. As demand for AI expertise has increased, the supply of qualified professionals has not kept pace, creating a talent gap that must be addressed. Solving this issue starts at the educational level, which we'll address in later chapters.

Another challenge is the ethical considerations surrounding AI. As AI becomes more prevalent in business operations, there is a growing need to ensure that the technology is used ethically and fairly. This includes addressing issues related to data privacy, bias, worker redundancy, and transparency.

In conclusion, AI has become a game-changing technology that is transforming the business world. The ability to process large amounts of data quickly and accurately, automate processes, and improve decision making has made AI a top priority for businesses across all industries. However, the challenges associated with implementing AI must be addressed in order to fully realize its potential as a strategic advantage.

Book Overview:

"AI Business Strategies" is a comprehensive guide to using artificial intelligence (AI) as a strategic tool for business success. The book provides a practical framework for understanding the potential benefits of AI and how businesses can use it to gain a competitive advantage.

The five main benefits to reading and understanding this book are:

Improved Efficiency

One of the primary benefits of using AI as a strategic advantage is improved business efficiency. By automating routine tasks and processes intelligently, businesses can reduce the amount of time and resources required to complete them. For example, AI-powered chatbots can handle customer inquiries, freeing up human customer service agents to focus on more complex issues. This isn't standard automation; it's *adaptive*. So as customer concerns change, so does the AI's handling of the issues. AI can also be used to automate supply chain management, reducing the amount of time required to manage inventory and order fulfillment.

Increased Accuracy

Another key benefit of using AI is increased accuracy. AI technologies are capable of processing vast amounts of data quickly and accurately, filtering out irrelevant noise and reducing the likelihood of errors. For example, AI can be used to analyze financial data, identify fraudulent transactions, and predict market trends with a high degree of accuracy. This can help businesses make more informed decisions and avoid costly mistakes.

Better Decision Making

AI can also be used to improve decision making by providing valuable insights and recommendations. For example, AI can be used to analyze customer data and provide personalized recommendations, improving the customer experience and driving sales. AI can also be used to analyze market trends and identify new opportunities, enabling businesses to pivot their strategies and stay ahead of the competition.

Cost Savings

AI can also help businesses save money by reducing the need for human labor in repetitive tasks and streamlining operations. By automating routine tasks, businesses can reduce labor costs, allow their existing workforce to focus on more important issues, and increase productivity. In addition, AI can be used to optimize processes and reduce waste, saving money on materials and resources.

Competitive Advantage

Finally, using AI as a strategic advantage can provide businesses with a significant competitive advantage, particularly if competitors aren't leveraging this technology. AI technologies allow businesses to differentiate themselves from the competition and offer better products and services. For example, AI can be used to improve product recommendations, offer personalized pricing, and enhance the overall customer experience.

The book is divided into four parts:

Part One provides an introduction to AI and its growing importance in the business world. It also explores the benefits of using AI as a strategic advantage, including improved efficiency, increased accuracy, better decision making, cost savings, and competitive advantage.

Part Two delves into the practical applications of AI in various industries, including finance, healthcare, retail, and manufacturing. It provides real-world examples of how businesses are using AI to drive innovation and gain a competitive edge.

Part Three focuses on the implementation of AI, including the challenges associated with integrating AI technologies into business operations. It also provides guidance on developing an AI strategy, building an AI team, and addressing ethical considerations related to AI.

Finally, Part Four looks to the future of AI and its potential impact on the business world. It explores emerging AI trends and technologies, such as deep learning and natural language processing, and provides insights into how businesses can stay ahead of the curve.

Overall, "AI Business Strategies" is a valuable resource for business leaders, managers, and professionals who want to understand the potential of AI and how to leverage it to achieve business success. The book is written in a clear, concise style and provides practical advice that can be applied to any industry.

"AI is like teenage sex: everyone talks about it, nobody really knows how to do it, everyone thinks everyone else is doing it, so everyone claims they are doing it too."

Dan Ariely, Behavioral Economist.

CHAPTER 2

Defining AI - Strong AI VS Weak AI

Artificial Intelligence (AI) is a broad term that encompasses a wide range of technologies and applications. At its core, AI is about developing machines and algorithms that can perform tasks that typically require human intelligence, such as learning, problem-solving, and decision making.

Are we talking about reducing human brains to nothing more than bytes and bits? Not exactly.

There are two types of AI that can be developed: **Strong AI** and **Weak AI**.

The definitions of Weak and Strong AI will differ depending on whether or not you're looking at the issue from a philosophical, technical, or practical point of view. *Strictly for the purposes of this book*, we'll assign the following definitions:

Strong AI is a program that has a mind in exactly the same sense human beings have minds. It thinks, reasons, and communicates in the same manner as human beings. It would be able to have a general, functional intelligence that could be applied to any issue. Whether or not sentience or consciousness is a component to Strong AI is up for debate. To date, no true Strong AIs have been created.

Weak AI is a program that ingests data and learns to perform a function within the narrow scope of its own code. It may be human-like, but it lacks the ability to transcend specific functions, whether those functions are directed or undirected. Its 'reasoning' is dictated strictly by the data that it ingests, not by any native or instinctual ability.

As of early 2023, all attempts at AI have resulted in the formation of a Weak AI, or no AI at all. The rough roadmap to reach the level of Strong AI is as follows:

Reactive Machines: Non-learning intelligence systems with static tasks. We've had these for decades. Aspects of facial recognition, pattern matching, and guided conversation fall into this category.

Limited Memory: Predictive modeling based on past experience. *This is the generation of AI that we're currently working with.* Every generation of this category of AI learns from past successes and mistakes, and is used to build something more efficient.

Theory of Mind: When an AI develops a combination of human emotions and personality traits, we will have reached the next level of AI. This generation of AI will use empathy and holistic thinking about the human condition to enhance its performance and usability.

Self Awareness: This generation of AI is the kind we see in many books and movies; they think, therefore they are. After mastering human emotions, AI in the final stage will recognise its own sentience, and act accordingly.

Keep all of this in mind when considering the implications of such technology, as it likely doesn't match the levels of AI displayed in popular science fiction, and proper expectations should be set when considering business changes and making proposals.

AI's Subfields

Let's explore the *five largest subfields of AI* and provide a high-level overview of their key characteristics and applications.

Machine Learning

Machine learning focuses on developing algorithms that can learn from data. In other words, the goal of machine learning is to build systems that can improve their performance over time based on experience. This is typically achieved through the use of statistical models and algorithms that are trained on large data sets. Machine learning has a wide range of applications, including image and speech recognition, natural language processing, creating computer controlled opponents in games and simulations, and predictive analytics.

Natural Language Processing

Natural Language Processing (NLP) allows computers to understand and interact with human language. This involves developing algorithms that can analyze and interpret human language in all its complexity, including its syntax, semantics, and pragmatics. NLP has a wide range of applications, including virtual assistants, chatbots, spycraft, and machine translation.

Computer Vision

Computer Vision is a subfield of AI that focuses on enabling machines to see and interpret the world in a way that is similar to human vision. This involves developing algorithms that can analyze and interpret visual information, including images and video. Computer vision has a wide range of applications, including autonomous vehicles, facial recognition, early warning systems, satellite image analysis, and medical diagnostics.

Robotics

Robotics allows developers to create machines that can interact with the physical world. This involves the creation of algorithms that can control and coordinate the actions of robots, enabling them to perform complex tasks such as assembly, resource harvesting, navigation, and manipulation. Robotics has a wide range of applications, including manufacturing, construction, healthcare, emergency rescue services, explosive ordinance disposal, and space exploration.

Expert Systems

Expert Systems is a subfield of AI that focuses on developing computer programs that can replicate the decision making capabilities of human experts in a particular domain. This involves capturing the knowledge and expertise of human experts and encoding it in a computer program. Expert systems have a wide range of applications, including automated software test design, medical diagnosis, financial planning, and engineering design.

In conclusion, AI is a broad and multifaceted field that encompasses a wide range of technologies and applications. Machine learning, natural language processing, computer vision, robotics, and expert systems are just a few of the key subfields of AI. By understanding the characteristics and applications of these subfields, businesses can begin to explore how AI can be used to achieve their strategic goals.

Different Types of AI Technologies

Artificial Intelligence (AI) is a rapidly evolving field, with new technologies and applications emerging on a regular basis. We will explore the most common types of AI technologies that are currently in use, providing an overview of their key characteristics and applications.

Rule-Based Systems

Rule-based systems are a type of AI technology that uses a set of predefined rules to make decisions or take actions. These rules are typically created by human experts in a particular domain and are encoded into a computer program. Most rule-based systems use some form of inference engine to interpret user input, classify it as a certain kind of issue, and then resolve that issue. Applications for AI systems include fraud detection, quality control, code compiling, and legal decision making.

Fuzzy Logic

Fuzzy Logic is designed to handle uncertain or imprecise information. Unlike traditional binary logic, which is based on a simple true/false decision making process, fuzzy logic allows for degrees of uncertainty and imprecision. Generally, it will weigh all of the factors of a given situation and then convert the results into a degree of certainty. That figure is used to chart a course towards issue resolution, using outcome tables. Fuzzy logic has a wide range of applications, including control systems, image processing, spelling and grammar checking, and decision making.

Genetic Algorithms

Genetic Algorithms are a type of AI technology that is inspired by the process of natural selection. The basic idea behind genetic algorithms is to create a population of potential solutions and then use a process of selection and recombination to evolve the best solutions over time. Each successive generation is given 'mutations' to see if performance improves or declines. The survivor of several rounds of selection is the optimal candidate. Genetic algorithms have applications that include optimization, scheduling, game theory, and design.

Neural Networks

Neural Networks are a type of AI technology that is inspired by the structure and function of the human brain. The basic idea behind neural networks is to create a network of interconnected nodes that can learn from data and make predictions based on that data. This is one of the largest 'umbrellas' of AI technology, with over a dozen core models that utilize techniques such as supervised learning, unsupervised learning, reinforcement learning, deep learning, and self-learning. Neural networks have a wide range of applications, including image and speech recognition, natural language processing, robotics, game AI, predictive analytics, autonomous vehicles, medical diagnosis, and natural language processing.

As you can see, AI is a broad and multifaceted field. Developers can adopt a wide range of techniques and code bases, creating bespoke solutions for their particular industry. Combinations of these technologies aren't uncommon either. For example, rule-based systems might be used during the data ingestion process, to determine what input is valid and filter out the rest. The result can then be fed to an unsupervised neural network, allowing it to learn and grow without exposing it to 'garbage' stimuli.

These are just a few of the key AI technologies that are currently in use. By understanding the characteristics and applications of these technologies, businesses can begin to explore how AI can be used to achieve their strategic goals.

Current Uses of AI

It's important to understand how AI is being applied across different industries and sectors, so that you can examine parallel applications in your own business. You don't want to reinvent the wheel, of course, but that's not the only reason. By delving deeper into specific scenarios that you might modify or adopt for your own needs, you can examine the technical, ethical, and practical hurdles that need to be overcome in order to have a successful AI implementation.

But let's start with some of the major AI implementations

seen in early 2023, to give you some scope as to how broad their application really is:

Healthcare

AI is being used in healthcare to improve patient outcomes, reduce costs, and increase efficiency. Some of the current uses of AI in healthcare include:

- Medical imaging: AI can help radiologists identify anomalies in medical images, such as X-rays and MRIs, more quickly and accurately than human experts. The NHS's National COVID-19 Chest Imaging Database (NCCID) is credited with saving thousands of lives by giving medical professionals and researchers free access to their AI breakdown of Covid-related lung conditions.

- Diagnosis and treatment: AI helps physicians diagnose and treat diseases, by analyzing patient data and recommending appropriate treatments. For example, Prevencio has two cardiovascular disease blood tests in labs right now, doing AI analysis of obstructive coronary artery disease as well as heart attack / stroke risk analysis.

- Drug discovery: Pharmaceutical companies identify new drug candidates more quickly and accurately using AI, by analyzing vast amounts of data. This phenomenon has inspired dozens of publications and an international conference on the subject.

- Telemedicine: By using cameras, sensors, and readily available tools and apps, doctors and nurse practitioners can do an analysis of a patient over the Internet. Incorporating AI into this process gives these medical professionals probability-based tools that can lead to surprising (and lifesaving) predictions about the future of a patient's health.

Finance

AI is being used in finance to improve risk management, fraud detection, and customer service. Some of the current uses of AI in finance include:

- Fraud detection: AI helps banks and other financial institutions identify fraudulent activity in a sea of hundreds of millions of mundane daily transactions. Additionally, back end analysis allows the detection of impersonation attacks on bank employees, as well as internal fraud.

- Credit scoring: Lenders use AI tools to assess creditworthiness more accurately, by analyzing a wider range of data sources than the major credit agencies track. This has made a large impact on credit underwriting, including the risk analysis of brand-new clients who have little to no traditional credit history.

- Trading: AI can help traders make better investment decisions, by analyzing market data, performing rapid research, and identifying patterns. Over 60% of U.S. equity trading is now done with AI assistance or performed entirely by AI tools.

- Financial risk analysis: Market contagion and currency evaluation are both complex tasks that are tailor made for AI analysis. AI was used to predict the extended drop in the British pound on the international stage post-Brexit, steering currency investors towards more stable and lucrative alternatives.

Retail

AI is being used in retail to improve customer experience,

increase sales, and reduce costs. Some of the current uses of AI in retail include:

- Personalization: AI helps retailers by providing personalized recommendations to customers, based on their preferences and past behavior. In fact, some of this personalization had to be reigned in due to the results being too 'spooky' to the customer. But with proper implementation, AI can deliver higher yields and lower costs of conversion than traditional ad campaigns.

- Inventory management: AI can help retailers manage inventory more efficiently, by predicting demand and optimizing stock levels. It can also detect intentional 'stock out' attacks that attempt to reserve products in a retail cart system via fraudulent means.

- Customer service: AI provides better customer service to retail clients, by automating common tasks and providing quick and accurate responses to customer inquiries. It can also perform urgency and severity analysis, and quantify typical risks due to a product or service failure.

Transportation

AI is being used in transportation to improve safety, reduce congestion, and increase efficiency. Some of the current uses of AI in transportation include:

- Autonomous vehicles: AI is being used to develop self-driving cars, trucks, and drones, which have the potential to reduce accidents and increase efficiency. Honda and Mercedes-Benz used AI extensively to field their groundbreaking level 3 autonomy cars in Japan and the United States respectively.

- Traffic management: AI can help transportation

authorities manage traffic more effectively, by analyzing real-time data and predicting traffic patterns. This includes an ever-increasing role in safety functions such as air traffic control and dock management. Project Bluebird, run by NATS and The Alan Turing Institute, is currently doing full AI flight management trials in live airspace.

- Logistics: AI helps logistics companies to optimize routes and delivery schedules, reducing costs and increasing efficiency. It may seem like science fiction, but Amazon currently has over 200,000 AI controlled robots working in their warehouses around the world.

- Maintenance: Rather than rely on the frailty of human pride in a job well done, AI is boxing the standard for infrastructure analysis and maintenance scheduling. That way there's no ego involved, and things get repaired quickly while root cause analysis is conducted. Hong Kong's subway engineers have been using an AI task analysis and deployment system since 2014.

Manufacturing

AI is being used in manufacturing to improve quality, reduce defects, and increase efficiency. Some of the current uses of AI in manufacturing include:

- Predictive maintenance: AI can help manufacturers identify potential equipment failures before they occur, reducing downtime and maintenance costs. This practice also extends to military hardware. Carnegie Mellon University holds a contract with the U.S. military to increase the scope of AI in their aircraft predictive maintenance routines.

- Quality control: AI can identify defects and anomalies in

products, reducing waste and improving quality. This is particularly important in the chemical industry, where QC failures can be dangerous or deadly. One nitrous oxide manufacturer uses AI and a series of sensors to weigh each compressed container to see if it was filled to the correct volume, scan it for defects in three dimensions, and perform failure analysis before the product ever touches human hands.

- Production optimization: Manufacturers optimize production schedules and resource allocation using AI. This increases efficiency and reduces costs, and has the pleasant side effect of reducing workplace injury.

- Worker health: An AI analysis of common worker patterns and medical leave records can lead to the intelligent redesign of a factory's floor plan, or the automation of repetitive tasks. Collaborative robots or exoskeletons can be assigned to roles that the AI determines are particularly stressful, reducing injury risks and engendering employee loyalty.

AI is being used in a wide variety of ways across different industries and sectors. By understanding the current uses of AI, businesses can begin to explore how these technologies can be used to achieve their own strategic goals.

Future Applications of AI

Artificial Intelligence (AI) is still a relatively new technology, and its potential applications are rapidly expanding. Let's explore some of the future applications of AI, in sectors such as education, entertainment, agriculture, and more.

Education

As an elected schoolboard commission and someone married to an English school teacher, I follow the progress of AI in this field with great interest. AI is starting to revolutionize education, by providing personalized learning experiences, automating administrative tasks, and improving student outcomes. Some of the planned applications of AI in education include:

- Personalized learning: AI can aid teachers in providing personalized learning experiences to students. By analyzing student learning styles, preferences, and relative progress, the AI can make slight alterations in the presentation style and the learning medium for each individual. Docebo is one of the first contenders in this field, starting with corporate training programs before they branch out into the larger educational arena.

- Assessment and grading: AI can help automate the assessment and grading of student work, reducing the workload for teachers and improving accuracy. Companies such as Graide have started to offer AI paper reviews, feedback suggestions, and grading tools that educators can use to streamline the process.

- Content creation: AI can be used to create and curate educational content, such as quizzes and study guides, based on student needs and preferences. Students that don't 'test well' often have the knowledge that is being asked of them, but aren't being asked the right questions. Age of Learning is one of the companies that is using AI to develop foundational material for young minds.

- Workforce retraining and rehoming: As certain types of jobs become less needed, either because of technological advances or social changes, AI can help to identify a candidate's strengths and match them to a new field that they will flourish within. SkyHive is one AI driven job search and analysis engine that will perform a gap analysis between a client and a job role, and suggest the right retraining regimen that will allow them to bridge the gap between industries.

Entertainment

AI has the potential to enhance the entertainment industry, by creating new experiences, improving audience engagement, and reducing production costs. Some of the future applications of AI in entertainment include:

- Content creation: AI can help create music, movies, and other forms of media, by analyzing patterns and preferences in existing content. Some great examples of this are currently being piloted on streaming services such as Twitch. UnlimitedSteam generates strange cooking based scripts involving two minor characters from The Simpsons, for example.

- Interactive experiences: AI can help create interactive experiences, such as virtual reality and augmented reality, that engage audiences in new and exciting ways. An example of this is the new AR app Weird Type, developed by Zach Lieberman and Molmol Kuo. By allowing AI to find and implement a convenient 'canvas' on the fly, participants can animate and write on anything within the virtual environment.

- Personalized recommendations: AI can help provide personalized recommendations for movies, music, and other forms of entertainment, based on user preferences and behavior. Sky TV in the UK is correlating moods to frequently used keywords, in an attempt to recommend content based on how the viewer is feeling at that particular moment, as part of a machine learning project spearheaded by Doctor Jian Li.

- Situational composition: Can music be composed on the fly to fit a particular situation within an open world video game? AAA gaming studios are currently experimenting with the idea, allowing generative AI to modify existing tracks and even create brand new ones based on any particular encounter.

Agriculture

AI has the potential to improve agriculture, by increasing crop yields, reducing waste, and improving sustainability. Some of the future applications of AI in agriculture include:

- Precision farming: AI can help farmers optimize crop planting, irrigation, and fertilization by analyzing data on soil conditions and weather patterns. This can help them come up with an optimal crop rotation, maintaining a good balance of soil nutrients for future planting needs. Aibono's AI analytics is an early implementation of this technology, using IoT devices and retailer consumption data to drive future planting and land management decisions.

- Pest and disease management: Identifying and managing pests and diseases is a high priority for farms of all sizes. By analyzing data on crop health, herd health, and environmental conditions with AI, highly targeted solutions can be delivered to the areas of the farm that need them the most. This helps farmers avoid the overuse of pesticides and antibiotics, saving money and improving yields.

- Crop monitoring: AI helps farmers monitor crop growth and health, by analyzing data from sensors and drones. Drone AI for orchard and vineyard monitoring is one of the hottest fields of study in agricultural management right now, and will likely lead to more general purpose applications in the near future.

- Environmental monitoring: Satellite and weather balloon imagery is rarely analyzed by hand these days. The impacts of erosion and climate change can be calculated and forecasted by mass image ingestion, and warnings sent out several months or years in advance of an impending environmental disaster. The United Nations Environment Program's (UNEP's) Digital Transformation team is pioneering new AI analytics that will help provide an early warning system for at-risk populations.

Energy

AI is going to transform the energy industry by optimizing energy production and distribution, reducing waste, and improving sustainability. Some of the future applications of AI in energy include:

- Smart grid management: AI will help utilities optimize energy production and distribution, by analyzing data on energy usage and supply. This is set to be one of the most massive integrations between AI systems and the IoT, one that needs to factor in literally billions of nodes. Expect several advancements along these lines over the next decade.

- Energy storage: Improving the efficiency and effectiveness of energy storage systems is one of the most critical challenges of the early 21st century. By predicting demand and optimizing usage, AI can help us tackle this issue. ABB is one of the companies pioneering fully digitalized energy storage portfolios, tackling storage infrastructure ranging from EV charging grids to gravity storage control systems.

- Renewable energy: AI can help improve the efficiency and effectiveness of renewable energy systems, such as solar and wind power, by predicting output and optimizing usage. Solar farms in particular are racing to embrace AI management, which is proving to minimize site build costs and optimize yields.

- Smart buildings: One of the earliest adopters of automation, the smart building industry, is also quick to embrace the AI revolution. ARUP's Neuron application is making use of IoT sensor data to do predictive building management. Trend analysis and environmental forecasting allows them to achieve a great balance between occupant comfort and energy usage.

Non-Profits

One of the biggest beneficiaries in the AI age will be non-profits. By improving the ability to track and respond to the causes that these organizations champion, a higher percentage of donated goods and funds will reach the targeted population centers. Some future applications of AI in the non-profit arena include:

- Personal appeals: Just as AI can help advertising companies to target their potential clients, AI analytics can help identify what motivates donors and create custom campaigns that will result in maximum generosity. The AI For Good Foundation identifies trends in humanitarian aid and helps organizations reach out effectively to donors in times of great need.

- Poaching and deforestation: AI can help organizations identify illegal activity that preys upon animal sanctuaries, endangered wildlife, and protected woodlands. An early implementation of this technology is Microsoft's Imazon, which uses satellite imagery to track and report illegal roads cut into the Amazon rainforest for logging and illicit agricultural operations.

. Public safety: AI can be used to rapidly analyze and react to public health crises. The first time this was used in a pandemic situation was during the recent Covid-19 outbreak, when the University of Aberdeen and the United Nations partnered to create ground-breaking antibody tests that were made available to the public in record time.

. Ethics: Lest we slip into murky waters, there needs to be guidelines that apply to AI development and implementation. Luckily, we have AI to help us do just that! Groups such as AI4ALL are establishing guidelines that will make sure that things like image and voice recognition apply equally across racial phenotypes and are tackling the ethical issues that arise as a result of AI usage.

As you can see, the potential applications of AI are enormous, and rapidly expanding. Businesses and industries should be exploring how these technologies can be used to achieve their strategic goals.

AI and Copyright - A Double Edged Sword

On one hand, *AI is great at protecting existing copyright and trademark claims*. It's a component of several popular intellectual property suites, attempting to detect whether or not protected works are being used without permission.

But as far as an AIs ability to *produce* a work that can be copyrighted, that's a whole different kettle of fish.

In the USA, AIs are not seen as entities that can hold a copyright. Nor can the direct product of their work be held by a third party as a copyrighted work. In the EU, only humans can produce a 'work'. Therefore, AIs cannot directly produce something that can hold copyright.

This all changes when **human editing** becomes involved. At that point, the edited version of the AIs work must be distinct enough from the original to be considered its own copyrightable entity. In other words, as long as the AI is used as a tool that creates a component of something else, and human hands go through the process of editing it to a sufficient degree, it would qualify for a potential copyright.

Please keep this in mind when you're making plans to incorporate AI into your creative portfolio! Simply generating and selling AI images online, branded onto products, or as prints does *not* protect you from copycats in much of the world. Unless the AI's work is heavily edited by a human being, it's fair game for anyone who wants to use it, at least as of early 2023.

"Artificial intelligence is the art of making computers that behave like they are smart, while in reality they are just following instructions."

Kevin Kelly, Co-founder of Wired magazine.

CHAPTER 3

Identifying Opportunities for AI

A rtificial Intelligence (AI) can provide businesses with a significant competitive advantage, but it's important to identify the right opportunities to apply AI technology. In this chapter, we will explore the step-by-step process of identifying opportunities for AI in business.

Learning AI's Limits

As much as everyone enjoys thinking outside the box, you need to understand what AI is good at, what it's bad at, and what it cannot do at all (in the present day, at least). Otherwise the opportunities that you identify might not be applicable to an AI model.

AI can't generate creativity, it can only take what it is given and change it in some way. To be useful it needs direction, both programmatically and artistically. It's horrible at making ethical decisions, so much so that random coin flips might be more appropriate. It doesn't understand every complexity that makes certain suggestions feasible and others completely impossible.

In short, AI is best used with specific guidance. And that guidance is applied both in the core code, and in choosing the data that it will ingest to come up with its conclusions.

Assessing Needs

The next step in identifying opportunities for AI is to assess your business's needs. This includes understanding your business objectives, identifying pain points or areas for improvement, and determining the potential impact of AI on these areas.

A few logical places to start include your primary revenue model, your largest areas of resources expenditure, your customer service, and your research division. These are likely to generate the biggest financial, reputational, and inspirational impacts to your business. After that, a key area to look at is employee satisfaction, training, health, and safety; because sharing the benefits of AI will help to win the support of your team members.

And you'll need that support. Because the AI implementation process will involve working with internal teams, bringing in external experts to work with them, and conducting market research to understand industry trends and best practices. Make sure to keep this in mind when assessing your business needs.

Analyzing Data

Once you have identified the areas of your business where AI could have the most impact, it's important to analyze your data to determine whether it's going to be suitable for AI ingestion. This step may uncover a lack of internal resources who are trained to assess AI data. If that's the case, pulling in qualified external resources or training the appropriate team members needs to happen immediately.

The AI ingestion process requires strict data governance. If you allow garbage data into the system, it might be virtually impossible to untangle the warping effect it has upon the AI learning process. This includes regulatory compliance, respecting confidentiality, respecting copyright, scrubbing out offensive (racist, sexist, etc.) content, and vetting scientific sources.

After assessing the quality and quantity of your data, identifying any data gaps, and determining whether your data is structured or unstructured, you can set up an ingestion map or schema. This process may involve working with data scientists, IT teams, or external partners to identify the best approach to data analysis.

Evaluating Potential Solutions

Once you have assessed your needs and analyzed your data, it's time to evaluate potential AI solutions. This involves considering the various types of AI technologies available, and determining which technology best suits your needs.

It also involves evaluating the various vendors or partners that offer premade AI solutions, and determining which ones (if any) have the expertise, resources, and experience to help you achieve your business objectives at the right price point. The temptation to create a solution yourself might be strong, but often it makes more financial sense to use something that has already been packaged and tested.

Part of your evaluation needs to include development resources, testing resources, pricing processing and storage resources, researching the additional network appliances or edge networking setups that might be required, and getting theoretical buy-in from key team leaders.

Developing a Proof of Concept

Before implementing an AI solution in your business, it's important to develop a proof of concept to demonstrate the potential value and effectiveness of the solution. You will be testing the solution in a controlled environment, analyzing the results, and determining whether it meets your stated business objectives.

Proof of concepts vary wildly depending on the project that is being undertaken. It might be as simple as hooking up a rudimentary AI to a chat bot and quizzing it about the contents of an online FAQ. Or it might be as complex as ingesting data from local IoT devices to see what suggestions the AI makes about environmental controls.

The process may involve working with a pilot group of users or customers, and obtaining their feedback to refine the solution before implementing it more broadly. Whatever the proof of concept encapsulates, key decision makers and stakeholders need to agree that it is in a state where investing more time and money to upscale the AI is worthwhile. Otherwise, it needs to be refined and a new proof of concept needs to be run.

Implementing and Scaling

Once you have developed a successful proof of concept, it's time to implement and scale the AI solution in your business. That means working with your internal teams or external partners to integrate the solution into your existing systems and processes, training your employees to use the solution effectively, and monitoring its performance to ensure that it's meeting your business objectives.

As this is likely going to be a major and ongoing component to at least one business function, the AI needs to be integrated with your disaster recovery and business continuity plans. It needs to be backed up iteratively, so that if something goes wrong it can be rolled back to a sane state. And resources need to be assigned to quickly bring the system back up in case of a major cyber attack, natural disaster, or sudden change in network service.

Finally, planning for future expansion and growth is critical. You have a framework in place, which significantly lowers the costs and expertise requirements to launch your next AI driven initiative. This gives you the freedom to consider how you can leverage AI to drive even more innovation and differentiation in your industry.

Assessing Your Business Processes

and Operations for AI Application

Artificial Intelligence (AI) has the potential to transform the way businesses operate, from optimizing processes to delivering better customer experiences.

However, not all business processes and operations are equally suited for AI application. It's important to assess each process and operation carefully to determine whether AI can be effectively applied.

Here's a six step process that you can use when assessing business processes and operations for AI application, including identifying areas for improvement, evaluating the data requirements, and determining the potential impact of AI on the business:

Identify Potential Degree of Improvement

Step one is assessing how much a particular area of your business could benefit from AI. Some of the most proven areas where AI has been applied include customer service, supply chain management, marketing, and sales. Some of the most disastrous applications of AI involve trying to replace roles that require creativity, empathy, or artistry.

That's not to say AI is useless in these more 'human' roles, but it has to be *used as an aid - not a replacement*! Until we reach the 'Theory of Mind' stage of AI evolution (as explained in Chapter 2), a real person needs to guide any process that is supposed to invoke or control emotional reactions.

With this in mind, you want to analyze the business process at a few different levels: *Repetivity, data availability, information or memorization intensity, and potential for generational improvement.* Anything that scores high on these scales has a high potential degree of improvement. Anything scoring low on these scales is likely a bad candidate.

Evaluate the Data Requirements

Once you have identified the areas of your business that could benefit from AI, it's important to evaluate the data requirements for an AI application. This involves considering the type and quality of data that is needed to train AI models and algorithms, and determining whether your business has access to the necessary data. It may also involve assessing the quality and completeness of your data, and identifying any gaps or inconsistencies that could impact the accuracy and effectiveness of AI.

For example, subjects that aren't well documented that rely heavily on 'trade secrets' would be a bad candidate for AI applications. On the other hand, subjects that have extensive wikis and tutorials are excellent candidates. Similarly, if your data ingestion comes primarily from polls, sensors, IoT devices, or existing aggregate sites (news, videos, social media, etc.), your data requirements are far easier. Make sure that any commercial services that you plan to use are available in formats that are easy for your AI to ingest.

Determine the Potential Impact of AI

Now that you know your data requirements, it's important to determine the potential impact of AI on your business processes and operations. Consider and rate the benefits that AI can provide, such as increased efficiency, reduced costs, and improved customer experiences. Then weigh these benefits against the costs, time investments, and risks associated with implementing AI.

Remember that the highest potential impact comes from areas of the business that aren't optimal to begin with. Applying AI tech to your most successful, highest budget projects might not give you the best return on investment. Make sure that you also look at aspects of your business that have the highest upside, and the most room for improvement.

Don't neglect the human impact of an AI implementation. Will there be employee pushback? Would you expect any redundancies if the program is successful? How much training will be required to utilize the results of the AI? The answers to these questions can impact employee retention, public image, union involvement, and even government scrutiny. Make sure that you plan for any contingencies accordingly.

Evaluate Feasibility

After assessing the potential impact of AI on your business processes and operations, it's time to look at the feasibility of implementing the AI within your current org structure.

First, you need to look at the technical requirements: The need for data analysis prior to ingestion, Cloud computing power, bandwidth requirements (particularly if you're ingesting video content or wide ranging IoT data), and additional system administration and devops resources.

Then there are the organizational requirements: Employee training, change management, public relations and advertising changes, and any redundancy impact. Part of examining feasibility involves assessing the resources and capabilities of your internal teams and external partners, and determining whether they have the expertise and resources to implement AI effectively. If not, you need to determine if utilizing external resources is viable.

Develop a Roadmap

We've already talked about planning your proof of concept and moving into full implementation. But prior to that, you need to set a realistic budget and timescale for spinning up your first AI instance.

There are dozens of templates available online, depending

on the type of AI and the industry you're in. But they all have certain tasks in common:

- Set up a secure sandbox environment for AI development.
- Establish your code control base (versioning, continuous integration and deployment, etc.)
- Prepare your network for ingestion (firewall configuration, bandwidth, permissions, etc.)
- Establish regular backups of the code base
- Prepare and deliver AI training data
- Monitor progress and report to stakeholders

After all that is set up, you can start moving into the aforementioned proof of concept phase. If you don't have external help with your AI project, make sure that you research an industry-specific roadmap that you can modify for your particular purposes.

Monitor and Evaluate Performance

Once you have implemented AI in your business processes and operations, it's important to monitor and evaluate its performance regularly. There are three forms of monitoring and evaluation that you need to keep in mind.

First, you want to make sure that your AI project is using the estimated amount of resources (computing and human alike) so that it has room to grow, and so costs don't spiral out of control. This means setting up strict performance monitoring on the project's cloud servers. It also means that people who are working on the AI project need to submit realistic estimates on how much of their time they're dedicating to it, and what kind of external resources they're leveraging.

Effective performance is gauged by how well the AI is doing its job. Based on the data and feedback that you receive, you might need to make adjustments to the AI's data ingestion or processing.

Continually optimizing your AI solution will ensure that it's providing the greatest possible value to your business.

Finally, you'll need to track the impact of AI on your business processes and operations, including the benefits and costs. Only then can you identify areas for improvement.

Assessing business processes and operations for AI applications requires a structured and analytical approach. By following the process outlined above, businesses can identify the right opportunities for AI, and achieve significant competitive advantages in their verticals.

"AI is the only field where a complete idiot can pretend to be an expert by creating a bot that pretends to be an expert."

Andrej Karpathy, Director of AI at Tesla.

CHAPTER 4

AI use Cases

I t might be helpful, at least for some readers, to go over some of the AI use cases that are out in the wild as of early 2023. Use cases can help businesses identify exact AI applications that they can implement, or give them ideas that they can modify to fit their own business situation.

AI Use Cases in Agriculture

The agricultural industry is one of the largest verticals in the world. It's seen significant advancements in technology in recent years, thanks to IoT and drone usage. Artificial Intelligence (AI) is one of the latest technologies to be adopted in agriculture, and it has the potential to transform the industry completely. By improving efficiency, reducing costs, and increasing yields, agriculture can be greener, more profitable, and friendlier to the local populace.

Here are some of the agricultural AI use cases seen in recent years:

Precision Farming

Precision farming involves using AI to optimize the use of resources, such as water, fertilizer, and pesticides, by analyzing data from sensors and other sources to determine the specific needs of each plant or crop. This can significantly reduce waste and improve yields, as well as improve sustainability by reducing the impact of farming on the environment. Precision farming can also help farmers identify potential problems early on, such as disease or pests, and take action to prevent or mitigate them.

An example of precision farming is the cutting-edge field of mistponics, also known as fogponics. Did I just make that word up? Sadly, no. An analysis is done on how well plants grow when sustained by various types of nutrient enriched fog. Because plant roots have specific 'gateways' for nutrition that can be measured down to the micron level, the types and concentrations of effective mists will vary by species. AI processes mix and deploy the feeding mists, and track the progress of plants exposed to certain concentrations and droplet sizes. Yields are most often significantly larger than hydroponics, with an overall decrease in energy usage.

Crop Monitoring

Crop monitoring is another use case for AI in agriculture, which involves using AI to monitor and analyze data from sensors and other sources to track the growth and health of crops. This can help farmers identify potential issues, such as nutrient deficiencies, pests, or disease, and take action to address them before they become significant problems. Crop monitoring can also help farmers make more informed decisions about when to harvest, based on the quality and maturity of the crops.

One surprising side effect of AI crop monitoring has been within the agrisolar movement. As AI started pointing out that certain types of plants and animals thrive in partial shade, more and more farmland was identified as prime mixed use property. The farmers could place rows of elevated solar panels in their fields, creating rows of shade while the AI managed solar arrays still produced around 80% of traditional solar yield. Crops and livestock thrived under these conditions, creating an amazing win-win scenario.

Livestock Management

AI can also be used to manage livestock, by analyzing

data from sensors and other sources to monitor the health and well-being of the animals, and identify potential issues before they become significant problems. This process can include monitoring the temperature, humidity, and air quality of livestock facilities, as well as tracking the movement and behavior of animals to identify signs of stress or illness. AI can also be used to optimize feed and water intake, and improve breeding and reproduction rates.

In addition to the aforementioned agrisolar projects, AI livestock management is discovering new ways for ranchers, livestock, and local predators to live together in harmony. The WildEyes AI field camera can identify individual wolves out of a pack. After tabulating their movement and potential territorial reach, The AI automatically alerts ranchers of the intrusion and activates deterrents to scare off the interloping wolves.

Predictive Analytics

Another use case for AI in agriculture is predictive analytics. This involves using data from sensors and other sources to forecast crop yields, identify potential risks, and optimize farm management strategies. This helps farmers to make more informed decisions about when to plant, fertilize, and harvest crops. These decisions are based on weather patterns, soil quality, market predictions, and several other factors. Predictive analytics can also help farmers identify opportunities for cost savings, such as by reducing waste or optimizing irrigation.

An interesting subset of agricultural predictive analytics is ROI tracking. By looking at a farmer's return on investment for every field, the AI can help plan crop rotations, rest seasons, or even suggest crop diversifications that might help correct the situation. This has given rise to shifting certain fields over to solar production, biomass production such as giant miscanthus, or dedicating them to hosting saplings that will be transplanted as part of tree planting initiatives.

Autonomous Farming

Autonomous farming is a rapidly developing use case for AI in agriculture. It involves using self-driving tractors and other equipment to perform tasks such as planting, fertilizing, and harvesting crops. This was famously featured in the 2014 film *Interstellar*.

AI can significantly reduce the need for manual labor, and increase efficiency, safety, and productivity on farms. Autonomous farming can also help lessen the impact of farming on the environment, by reducing emissions and waste. Bear Flag Robotics, recently bought by John Deere, is one of the pioneers in this area, rapidly rolling out fleets of autonomous tractors across the USA.

AI Use Cases in Automotive

The automotive industry has been experiencing a painful rebirth in recent years, as vital microchips were in short supply and production levels crashed during the Covid pandemic. AI was one saving grace that allowed the industry to transform in these harsh times. By improving safety, efficiency, and the customer experience, AI has helped set the auto industry on a more profitable, environmentally friendly path.

Autonomous Vehicles

Autonomous vehicles are one of the most promising use cases for AI in the automotive industry, and they are expected to revolutionize transportation in the coming years. Autonomous vehicles use AI to analyze data from sensors and other sources to make decisions about steering, acceleration, and braking, without human intervention. They can also calculate optimal routes, refueling or recharging points, and maintenance schedules. This technology can significantly improve safety, reduce accidents caused by human error, and optimize traffic flow.

In 2021, Mercedes and Honda were the first companies to roll out a Level 3 Autonomy car to their respective markets. In congested traffic and while waiting in lines, the driver doesn't need to have their hands on the wheel. This is the first major step forward in the race to full autonomy.

Predictive Maintenance

Another use case for AI in the automotive industry is predictive maintenance, which involves using AI to analyze data from sensors and other sources to forecast when maintenance will be required on vehicles. Similar to factory applications, the advantage that vehicles have over industrial machines is that they're already tied into a sophisticated web of internal sensors.

This can help manufacturers and dealerships identify potential issues before they become significant problems, and take action to prevent them from occurring. Predictive maintenance can also help reduce costs by optimizing maintenance schedules and reducing downtime.

Customer Engagement

AI can also be used to improve customer engagement in the automotive industry, by analyzing data from social media, customer reviews, and other sources to identify customer preferences and sentiment. This can help manufacturers and dealerships develop more targeted marketing campaigns, and tailor products and services to meet the specific needs of their customers.

Cerebri AI is one of the firms focusing on auto industry customer engagement. They're making sure that offers sent to clients are less likely to upset them, for example, by filtering out offers to clients who have just spent money that would have been saved if they had waited a couple of weeks. Reducing customer regret is a major part of what AI accomplishes in this role.

Intelligent Transportation Systems

Intelligent Transportation Systems (ITS) involves using AI to optimize traffic flow, improve safety, and reduce emissions. ITS can include technologies such as adaptive cruise control, lane departure warning, swarm navigation, and traffic sign recognition. These technologies use AI to analyze data from sensors and other sources to make decisions about driving behavior, and communicate with other vehicles and infrastructure to optimize traffic flow.

One of the earliest adopters of this technology was Google Maps. By taking reports about traffic conditions, traffic flow disruptions, and alternative routes, they're able to verify their authenticity and then push out live updates to their users. This enhances and informs GPS guided routing, and helps both commuters and emergency services get where they need to go.

Supply Chain Optimization

AI is often used to optimize the supply chain in the automotive industry. By analyzing data from suppliers and logistics providers, manufacturers can identify potential bottlenecks and optimize production schedules. This helps reduce costs, improve efficiency, and reduce procurement lead times. AI can also be used to optimize inventory management, by forecasting demand and ensuring the availability of parts and components when they are needed.

AI could have helped to lessen the impact of the global automotive chip shortage during the Covid pandemic. Analysts on the SIA have demonstrated that AI can be used to suggest optimal parts inventory levels for 'black swan events'. Had the major manufacturers adopted these AI strategies, they would have been in a much better market position.

AI Use Cases in the Call Center Industry and IT Support

The call center industry has been in a downward spiral for the past two decades, with a recent survey finding that only 24% of customers are satisfied with the level of customer service they receive. But AI is starting to turn those trends around. AI technology is playing a significant role in improving customer experience, enhancing efficiency, and reducing costs. Some of the implementations of AI include:

Chatbots

A promising use case for AI in the call center industry is chatbots, which are virtual assistants that can interact with customers through text-based messaging. Chatbots use AI to analyze customer requests, respond with relevant information, and provide personalized recommendations. This can help reduce wait times, improve customer satisfaction, and reduce costs by automating repetitive tasks.

OpenDialog is currently being used on support websites throughout the world. Its code is freely available on GitHub, allowing developers to integrate custom chatbot support solutions quickly. The conversational agents are accessed via a user-first UI, and can be 'programmed' by non-techies, requiring no coding experience.

Voice Assistants

Another use case for AI in the call center industry is voice assistants, which use AI to analyze customer requests and provide relevant information through voice-based interactions. Voice assistants can be integrated into call center systems, allowing customers to speak to a virtual assistant to get help with their inquiries. This reduces wait times and provides a more personalized experience for customers. It can also route people to the right departments far more reliably than numerical option menuing.

Turnover in call centers is high, and experience doesn't

always get passed down efficiently. AI can help bridge the experience gap by doing comprehensive analysis of things like customer problem history, correlation of call volume to certain IoT events such as device outages, and skipping first level support when the issue is clearly more advanced or beyond the authority of a level one agent.

Predictive Analytics

AI can be used to analyze data from call center interactions to identify patterns and make predictions about customer behavior. This can help call center agents provide more personalized service, by anticipating the needs of the customer and providing targeted recommendations. Predictive analytics can also help call center managers optimize operations by identifying bottlenecks and areas for improvement.

In 2023, Gartner put Google at the top of the list for conversational AI platforms using predictive analytics. Their call center AI can quickly pick out key call drivers on the fly, gauge customer urgency, and find common threads between incoming calls. This empowers management to quickly activate additional remote resources as needed, and report critical issues to IT in real time.

Sentiment Analysis

Another use case for AI in the call center industry is sentiment analysis. This involves analyzing the tone and emotion of customer interactions to identify customer satisfaction levels without the need for polling. Sentiment analysis can help call center managers understand the customer experience, provide more personalized service, and identify areas for improvement.

Sentiment analysis can be used, for example, to see how upset a customer is during the AI prescreening of their call. By the time the client is routed to the correct department, the AI will have some idea if they need to be treated with 'kid gloves' or not.

This kind of system can be gamed, however, by clever clients who just want faster support service.

Customer Journey Analytics

Analysis of the customer journey by an AI system is an important step towards understanding how efficiently customers flow through the system, and how happy they are along the way. From initial contact to resolution, AI can be used to identify areas where improvements can be made. By analyzing data from multiple touchpoints, call center managers can gain insight into the customer experience and identify opportunities to provide more streamlined or personalized service. This can help improve customer satisfaction and reduce churn.

Amplitude is one of the platforms being used by major tech companies to perform AI mapping of the customer journey. The theory is that people often don't state what they want, they make statements that they believe will *result* in what they want. By using A/B testing under AI scrutiny, the effectiveness of the customer journey is actually tested, and customer statements are broken down to analyze what their end goal really is.

AI Use Cases in Education

AI can transform the education sector more quickly than just about any other industry. That's because the transfer of knowledge via textual, video, and vocal mediums is AI's bread and butter. The potential for AI to revolutionize the way students learn, how teachers and administrators manage the education system, and how parents understand and enhance the learning process is immeasurable.

Personalized Learning

By analyzing data such as a student's learning history, performance, and interests, AI algorithms can create customized learning paths for each student. This can help to improve student engagement and achievement levels. Such techniques have already been proven in areas such as web security training, and the lessons learned from those activities are being filtered down to traditional education sectors.

The prediction of personalized learning was crystalized in Neal Stephenson's novel *The Diamond Age* with the concept of the 'illustrated primer'. With mobile devices becoming ubiquitous, science fiction is rapidly becoming science fact. The Learning Guild is already tracking AI learning solutions that will customize lessons for each student, and identifying the most cost effective packages for mass rollout. Personalized learning is swiftly becoming a matter of political will, rather than financial or technological barriers.

Automated Grading

AI can be used to automate grading for multiple choice and objective questions, freeing up teachers to focus on other areas of assessment. This can save teachers significant time and help to reduce grading bias.

Versions of the multiple-choice automatic checker have existed for decades, with Scantron leading the way some fifty years ago. But cheaper home-based systems using readily available webcams or mobile devices are invaluable to educators everywhere. Similarly, OCR has been around forever, but AI's ability to gain an understanding of the context of answers allows it to parse things other than true, false, or the exact textbook wording of something.

Chatbots for Student Support

AI-powered chatbots can provide 24/7 support to students. They can answer frequently asked questions and provide guidance on various topics, such as enrollment, academic advising, and financial aid. This can help to reduce the workload on administrative staff and improve the overall student experience.

We're not talking about ChatGPT passing an MBA exam at Wharton... though that did happen in March 2023. Instead, the intended role of AI would be to point students towards study resources, campus aid, and events that would be of some interest. Reducing feelings of helplessness or alienation goes a long way towards developing successful study habits.

Predictive Analytics for Student Intervention

AI can be used to predict student performance, behavior, and outcomes. This can help educators to identify struggling students early on and provide targeted support, as well as predict which students are likely to excel in certain subjects or fields.

The Elman neural network developed at the University in Indonesia can use a student's record and their preferences to match them with an internship placement that will be somewhat challenging, and yet still within their capabilities. This is the first of many AI tools that can be used to help guide academic progress and oversee the transition of a student from academia to the working world.

AI Use Cases in Remote Medicine

AI is increasingly being used in the healthcare sector, and with the rise of remote medicine, its potential applications are even more significant. Remote medicine involves the use of technology to provide healthcare services to patients who are not physically present in the same location as the healthcare provider. Here are some of the more common use cases of AI in modern medicine:

Telemedicine

AI can be used to analyze images and biomonitoring data, then provide remote consultation and diagnosis. By using AI-powered chatbots and virtual assistants, patients can have access to 24/7 healthcare support and guidance, reducing the burden on healthcare providers. AI can also act as a 'triage' mechanism, routing low risk health issues into over the counter or delivery prescription services, and routing more serious issues to specialist or emergency services.

Increasingly, telemedicine is being used as a cost and time saving measure that also dramatically increases the quality of life for rural and low-income households. The U.S. government's HHS division offers AI assisted telehealth checkups covering Ear/Nose/Throat, Skin, Abdominal, Cardiopulmonary, Neurological, and Musculoskeletal issues.

Remote Monitoring

AI-powered devices can be used to remotely monitor patients' health, providing real-time data on vital signs, activity levels, and other health metrics. This can help healthcare providers to detect potential health issues early on and provide targeted support.

Philips in the Netherlands is currently using wearable sensors to transition low risk patients from in-patient to out-patient care. The device does an analysis every five minutes for fourteen days, and reports on any abnormalities. In this way, vitals and biochemistry can be monitored in the comfort of the patient's own home, freeing up bed space for more critical cases.

Diagnostic Imaging

AI can be used to analyze medical images, such as X-rays, CT scans, and MRIs, providing faster and more accurate diagnoses. This can help to reduce the time and cost associated with manual interpretation of medical images.

It can also make some amazing correlations that find issues that traditional exams wouldn't. Tulane University researchers found that AI can accurately detect and diagnose colorectal cancer. AI analysis of tissue scans was on par with or better than the results provided by pathologists acting alone.

Drug Discovery

If you need to analyze large amounts of medical data, such as patient records and scientific literature, in order to identify potential drug candidates, AI is the perfect medium. This can help to speed up the drug discovery process and provide more effective treatments for patients.

Exscientia is using AI to create highly targeted drugs that can work with the patient's immune system and design custom molecules that only bind to the areas that need medical attention. They use every new molecule to either green light or eliminate the next series of trials, rapidly narrowing down the scope of the research.

Predictive Analytics

AI can be used to predict patient outcomes and identify patients who are at high risk of developing certain conditions. This can help healthcare providers to develop personalized treatment plans and provide targeted support to high-risk patients.

The British Journal of Ophthalmology published a paper in late 2022 that detailed how AI can accurately predict heart disease risk via a one-minute eye scan. This is an incredibly low-cost mitigation when compared to the cost of cardiovascular interventions.

Intelligent Medical Devices

AI can be used to power intelligent medical devices, such as prosthetics, pacemakers, and insulin pumps. These devices can adapt to a patient's specific needs and provide personalized care and support.

In 2022, development of an AI powered artificial pancreas revolutionized diabetes management. Funding for a global rollout of this MedTech development is ongoing, but the quality-of-life increases, particularly in areas with high obesity, are incredible.

AI Use Cases in the Financial Industry

The financial industry is one of the most significant industries in the world for the integration of Artificial Intelligence. Let's explore some of the use cases of AI in this vertical.

Fraud Detection

AI can be used to detect fraudulent activities in real-time. The analysis of massive data streams can identify unusual patterns of activity, and flag them for human review. In the case of obvious fraud, the entire system can be automated, and only the appeals process would require human intervention. This helps financial institutions prevent fraudulent transactions and protect their customers from financial loss.

HUMAN is a security company offering cutting edge AI fraud detection and mitigation. Their algorithms can detect stock-out attacks, price manipulation, false account creation attempts, and other financial attacks. This helps banks, credit institutions, and insurance.

Customer Service

AI provides customer support and client engagement in the financial industry. AI-powered chatbots and virtual assistants can help customers with basic queries, account management, and other services, providing 24/7 support without the need for human intervention.

Automation of things like checking account balance, security checks, and basic authorizations have been around for years. What AI has done is increased the scope of self-service options dramatically. Everything from setting contingency-based trades to arranging escrow is now possible without agent intervention, which speeds up customer fulfillment and lessens the burden on support professionals.

Investment Management

Portfolio management using AI can provide better analysis and investment recommendations because AI can ingest market data at a global level. This allows the AI to identify patterns that humans might not see, and make investment decisions that are more precise and reliable.

Portfolio managers are using NLP/G engines to do industry-specific analyses and to find the traits that are reliable markers for future success. Though there's no such thing as a sure thing, a shift of just one or two percentage points can mean a shift of billions of dollars for their clients.

Risk Management

AI can be used in risk management roles to analyze financial risks and provide recommendations for reducing exposure. AI-powered systems can analyze data from multiple sources, pinpoint risk factors, suggest mitigation, and provide real-time insights for better decision making.

Perhaps one of the earliest adopters of AI risk management as it applies to the financial services fields is big consultancy. Deloitte, PWC, and KPMG all have aggressive AI analysis tools that they use for both auditing and exposure testing.

Credit Scoring

AI can be used to provide more accurate credit scoring. AI-powered systems can analyze massive amounts of data from multiple sources, including social media and other digital footprints, to provide more accurate credit scores, reducing the risk of fraud and increasing the accuracy of lending decisions.

H2O AI is just one of the firms that have designed neural network AIs that improve the credit scoring process for clients. Credit score model building for new financial products now takes days instead of months. Tighter acceptance windows saved clients tens of millions of dollars. And the robust reporting features save hundreds of hours of work per human underwriter. These benefits are commonly seen in other AI credit scoring companies, and should be the expected norm these days.

Anti-Money Laundering (AML)

AML is critical to both government compliance and the long term financial health of a financial services company. AI can be used to detect money laundering, insider trading, social engineering, and other financial crimes.

C3's AI has been used in AML applications. One of the most impressive statistics that their clients have shared is an 85% reduction in false-positive alerts. That represents a big time savings to the anti-money laundering investigations team. The real-time risk profiles become more accurate and the reporting far more in depth when compared to human agents, who in the past had to make snap decisions with far too little information on hand.

AI Use Cases in the Transportation Industry

The transportation industry is a vital part of our society and economy, and it has been undergoing significant changes with the integration of Artificial Intelligence (AI). The primary concerns that AI is addressing in this vertical are safety or logistics related, but there is a myriad of problems that can be tackled with emerging technology:

Autonomous Vehicles

One of the most significant use cases of AI in the transportation industry is the development of autonomous vehicles. AI-powered systems can analyze data from sensors and cameras in real-time, making decisions on steering, acceleration, and braking, and allowing vehicles to operate with minimal human intervention. In the near future, we'll likely see fully autonomous vehicles that will function with no human intervention at all.

Stage 4 autonomous driving is coming along rapidly in 2023. There are already several autonomous car hire services, also known as 'robo-taxis', operating throughout the world. Baidu and WeRide are already well established in parts of China. Waymo is operating autonomously in Arizona, and has applied for driverless permits in California's Bay Area.

Traffic Management

In order to manage traffic in real-time, an AI has to ingest an incredible amount of data from multiple sources: Traffic sensors, GPS, cameras, LIDAR stations, and social media to name a few. They use this data to provide real-time updates on traffic flow, congestion, and road conditions. This can help reduce traffic jams, improve safety, and optimize commutes.

In the UK, the Nottingham City Council has installed 219 sensors to implement the new VivaCity AI traffic management system. The AI will have control over traffic lights and ring road entry. The system can eventually tie into road safety services and public transport systems to optimize traffic flow.

Fleet Management

AI can be used in fleet management, providing real-time data on vehicle performance, fuel efficiency, logistics optimization, and maintenance requirements. This can help transportation companies fine tune their fleets, reduce costs, and improve safety.

In 2022, Amazon launched their Fleet Edge driver safety and route mapping system. It uses AI to not only create live maps of areas that can be used to detect dangerous or highly disruptive traffic issues, but to blur out faces and license plates so that individual privacy is maintained all the while.

Predictive Maintenance

Predictive maintenance is one of AI's strongest talents. By analyzing data from sensors and other sources to identify potential equipment failures before they occur, AI can help transportation companies reduce downtime, improve safety, and lower maintenance costs.

This technology is going beyond polling a vehicle's onboard sensors. Snapshots of the tires at rest can detect balding and underinflation before a driver even notices. Audible cues can be analyzed to see if they fit any common risk patterns seen in vehicles of that particular make and model. Even driver feedback can be taken into account, using the most subtle clues to examine potential issues before they become more severe.

Passenger Experience

AI can be used to enhance the passenger experience, providing real-time information on travel times, delays, and other factors that can impact them. This can help transportation companies provide better services and improve customer satisfaction.

Assistant professor Sharan Srinivas performed an AI analysis of around 400,000 publicly available customer reviews covering six of the major U.S. airlines. The AI suggested an 11 point plan to reduce customer dissatisfaction, revolving around more flexibility and greater personalization of the flight experience. Costs focused on one time expenditures that would provide long term benefits.

AI Use Cases for the Supply Chain

The supply chain is a complex network of activities that involves the planning, sourcing, manufacturing, and delivery of products or services to customers. The integration of Artificial Intelligence (AI) can help companies to optimize their supply chain operations and achieve significant competitive advantages. In this chapter, we will explore some of the use cases of AI in the supply chain.

Demand Forecasting

AI can be used to forecast demand accurately, analyzing historical sales data and other factors such as weather patterns, seasonal trends, and consumer behavior. This can help companies optimize their inventory levels, reduce waste, and improve profitability.

One of the biggest challenges to forecasting is selling a brand new product or service with no comparable industry history. AI can draw parallels between customer bases from similar industries to predict how something innovative will be received by the market.

Inventory Management

AI can be used for real-time inventory monitoring, using sensors, active labeling, and cameras to track inventory levels in real-time. This can help companies maintain optimal inventory levels, reduce stockouts, and avoid overstocking.

The ultimate marriage between big data and logistics is achieved by combining AI with Near Field Communication (NFC). The ability to 'gate' your inventory with NFC and track items precisely throughout a warehouse gives AI an incredible amount of information to work with. This allows for the fine tuning of product storage, with additional optimization available for forecasted demand during sales events.

Logistics Optimization

Logistics optimization consists of analyzing data from global sources to provide real-time insights. AI can use this data for route optimization, load balancing, and fine tuning the efficiency of transportation operations. The result is reduced costs, better quality of life for delivery drivers, and improved delivery times.

For example, AI has shown that allowing drivers to utilize the most comfortable routes and rest stops yields superior results, which also complies with national and regional work regulations. When driver preference is integrated into logistics priorities, the long-term benefits are excellent.

Supplier Management

AI can be used to monitor supplier performance, analyzing data on delivery times, quality, return rates, and pricing factors to identify potential issues before they occur. This can help companies to optimize their supplier relationships, reduce costs, and improve the quality of their products or services.

Supplier onboarding is one of the best uses for AI in the supply chain management spectrum. It can provide optimal documentation based on supplier feedback, specific instructions that are synchronized with contractual agreements, and learning tools that are personalized to the best way that individual third-party agents learn.

Predictive Maintenance

With the use of AI, data from sensors and other sources can be analyzed to detect potential equipment failures in advance. This technique can assist companies in reducing equipment downtime, enhancing safety, and decreasing maintenance expenses.

The use cases for this are the same as those noted for the automotive industry. Additionally, there are systems that can do an analysis of forklifts, warehouse exoskeletons, and bay doors in order to suggest maintenance steps and prevent catastrophic failure.

Quality Control

AI can be used for quality control, using sensors and cameras to monitor product quality in real-time. This can help companies identify defects and other issues before they reach the customer, improving customer satisfaction and reducing costs associated with returns and recalls.

QualityLine is one example of AI analytics software that predicts possible defects caused by the manufacturing process, and suggests measures to correct them. Its automated root cause analysis takes into account all supplier and manufacturer parameters.

AI Use Cases for Food Transformation Industry

The food transformation industry can benefit from a wide range of AI applications. Because most food has a finite shelf life, increasing the speed of food inspection and optimizing food processing will reduce waste and increase profitability. Some of the most common use cases include:

Quality Control

AI can be used to monitor and control the quality of food products, preventing foodborne illnesses and improving food safety. It detects defects and inconsistencies in food products, some of which are not visible to the human eye. The result is food waste reduction and higher customer satisfaction. The AI's scope extends to 'grading' certain kinds of produce more accurately, reducing product returns and increasing the ability to make crushed, dried, or liquified products such as juices, jams, instant mash, and slurries.

Much like we saw in supply chain QC, there are AI products for preventing food recalls as well! Agroknow is a company that specializes in predictive hazard detection that might cause food to be recalled. Their Ai tech is used by Hershey, Coca Cola, and Nestle among others.

Predictive Maintenance

As we've seen in other industries, AI can be used to predict equipment failures and perform maintenance tasks before they become critical. This can help reduce downtime and increase efficiency.

Using AI based predictive maintenance, processing and canning machines have seen a reduction in mean time to repair (MTTR) by around 60%.Oil build up patterns, surface temperature monitoring, and vibration analysis is used in tandem to detect early inefficiencies and correct them, thus preventing bigger issues down the line.

Personalized Nutrition

AI can be used to analyze an individual's genetic data, nutritional needs, and dietary preferences to provide personalized eating recommendations. This can help individuals make healthier food choices and reduce the risk of chronic ailments ranging from heart conditions to diabetes.

DayTwo, an AI based on research by Eran Elinav and Eran Segal, uses age, weight, microbiome profiles, blood sugar, medical history, and personal preferences to determine the optimal and most enjoyable diet for each individual user. It's just one example of an entirely new sector of the AI food app industry.

Flavor and Texture Optimization

AI is already being used to optimize the flavor and texture of food products by analyzing data from sensory panels and other sources. This can help improve the overall quality of food products and increase customer satisfaction.

Analytical Flavor Systems uses AI models to create a 'gastrographic' profile of flavor, aroma, and texture. Then they use subtle alterations and polling to more closely match the typical customer's food and drink preferences.

AI Use Cases for Energy Industry

By optimizing energy production, reducing operational costs, and improving environmental sustainability, AI is transforming the energy industry. Here are just some of the examples of AI's usage in the energy industry:

Demand Response

AI can be used to predict energy demand and adjust supply accordingly. This can help to balance the grid and reduce the risk of blackouts. Calculations have to include the response time of emergency power generation, the round trip efficiency of various energy storage types, regional and national special events, and grid efficiency ratings. All of these things can fluctuate over time, depending on local conditions, making this a particularly challenging task for humans without AI assistance.

The scientific work of Fridgen, Halbrügge, Körner, Michaelis, and Weibelzahl shows the massive scope of this issue in detail, and suggests the best ways for AI to tackle demand response in a holistic way. To date, no national grid has been able to fully implement such solutions, but initial steps are being made in Germany and Australia.

Renewable Energy Forecasting

Forecasting the output of renewable energy sources such as solar and wind is difficult even at the best of times. AI can help to integrate renewable energy into the grid more effectively, as well as plan for renewable expansion based on long term forecasts and the types of energy storage available in given areas.

One example of this is the SunShot Initiative, a joint IBM and US Department of Energy solar forecasting program. Predictions on solar generation have improved by over 30% thanks to the AI in question. These findings allow power plants to more accurately control production and save consumers and energy companies a lot of money in the long run.

Energy Trading

AI can be used to optimize energy trading by predicting market trends and identifying profitable opportunities. The aforementioned forecasting improvements also translate to more well-informed short and long term investments.

Veos Digital is one of the AI As A Service companies offering on demand energy trading intelligence. Using their systems, an energy trader can fully automate the trading process (algo-trading) by providing the AI a dedicated fund to trade with.

Energy Efficiency

AI can be used to optimize energy usage in buildings and industrial facilities, reducing energy consumption and costs.

Carbon Capture

The process of capturing and storing carbon emissions is complex under the best circumstances. AI can help to predict sequestering tactics that will work in the long term, without the need for human trust (which is the case with any forestry-based project). This can help to reduce the environmental impact of energy production.

The U-FNO system, an enhanced Fourier neural operator, simulates the kind of pressure found deep in porous rock formations. It can then suggest exactly where and how CO_2 should be introduced to these rock formations so that it is permanently trapped deep underground. This is just one of the cutting-edge AI modeling instances that is transforming the carbon capture industry.

Natural Language Processing

AI can be used to analyze text data such as reports and regulatory documents, allowing energy companies to stay up to date with industry developments and comply with regulations.

In September 2017, the FCA used AI to take their 20,000 pages of regulatory documents and transform them into a searchable, human language document and database. 3,000 metadata tags were identified and added to the raw legal text, and the reading order was logically streamlined.

"AI is not a silver bullet. It is more like a titanium spork: useful for a wide range of tasks, but not necessarily the best tool for every job."

Michael I. Jordan, Professor of Computer Science at UC Berkeley.

CHAPTER 5

Building an AI Team

B uilding an AI team is a crucial step for any organization that wants to develop and deploy artificial intelligence (AI) solutions. AI is a complex and rapidly evolving field, and creating a successful AI team requires a diverse set of skills and expertise. In this chapter, we will explore the key elements of building an AI team and the considerations that go into each element.

The steps to building an internal AI team will differ depending on whether this will be a temporary or permanent addition to your staff, whether management of the AI system will be in house or delegated to an external service, and what leadership's financial commitment is to the project. But generally speaking, these are the steps to consider:

1. **Identify Your Goals and Needs**: The first step in building an AI team is to identify your organization's goals and needs. What problem do you want to solve with AI? What kind of data do you have or need to collect? What kind of application or system do you want to build? Answering these questions will help you determine the skills and expertise required for your AI team. We cover a lot of this process in Chapter 3

2. **Hire the Right People**: The next step is to hire the right people. AI teams typically require a mix of technical and non-technical skills. Technical skills may include expertise in machine learning, data science, computer vision, natural language processing, or deep learning. Non-technical skills may include project management, communication, and business acumen.

   It's important to hire people who have experience working with the specific technologies and tools you plan to use. Look for candidates who have relevant academic or work experience, and who have demonstrated an ability to learn quickly and adapt to new technologies. If you can't find the right talent, you may need to consider outsourcing.

3.   **Create an Agile Development Environment**: AI projects are often complex and can take a long time to develop. Creating an agile development environment can help your team stay focused and productive, creating working models that will showcase progress to stakeholders. This may include regular check-ins and reviews, agile methodologies such as Scrum or Kanban, and the use of collaboration tools such as Jira or Trello.

It's important to note that at least one stakeholder has to be part of the Agile process. Without a stakeholder as a champion, most Agile projects fail. They don't need to be technical, but they need to be willing to have some degree of vocal advocacy. They need to believe in the project.

4.   **Foster a Culture of Learning**: The field of AI is constantly evolving, and it's important to foster a culture of learning within your team. Encourage your team members to attend conferences, participate in online courses, and read the latest research papers. Encourage experimentation and provide opportunities for your team to explore new technologies and tools.

5.   **Prioritize Data Quality and Privacy**: Data is the lifeblood of AI, and it's important to prioritize data quality and privacy. Your team should have a deep understanding of data governance and compliance, as well as data cleaning and preprocessing techniques. In addition, your team should be well-versed in the latest privacy regulations and best practices for data security.

We're going to go back to a central theme in this book: *Controlling your AI's data ingestion is critical*. It can mean the difference between a working model and a toy. It can mean the difference between a helpful, functional support chatbot and a racist one. We've all heard the tales of AI disasters resulting from the ingestion of garbage data. Don't become the next cautionary tale… or worse, the next darkly comedic headline story.

6.   **Provide the Right Tools and Infrastructure**: The success of your AI team depends on having the right tools and infrastructure in place. This may include access to cloud-based services such as AWS or Azure, development environments such as Jupyter or RStudio, and collaboration tools such as GitHub or GitLab.

For AI projects requiring real time multi-campus input, mass video or audio ingestion, or other bandwidth intensive activities, you need to examine your network infrastructure as well. Edge networking might be required to facilitate campus to campus communications or high speed backbone access to specific metropolitan area networks. The project also needs to play nicely with firewall rules, packet filters, and load balancers.

7.   **Encourage Collaboration and Diversity**: It's important to encourage collaboration and diversity within your AI team. This may include cross-functional training, team-building exercises, and opportunities for team members to share their expertise and knowledge. Encouraging diversity in terms of gender, race, and background can also help to foster creativity and innovation within your team.

AI has no human sensibilities. It doesn't understand issues like racism, sexism, or prejudice. A deeply homogenized team might accidentally produce an AI that only takes into account a single outlook or lifestyle, which can not only lead to something like a racist chatbot, but can have impacts on everything from facial recognition to natural language parsing. Diversity in AI development isn't just a buzzword, it's a realistic necessity.

Building an AI team requires a mix of skills and a focus on collaboration, learning, and diversity. By following these guidelines, you can build a successful AI team that can help your organization to solve complex problems and drive innovation.

Recruiting and hiring the right talent

Recruiting and hiring the right talent for an AI project is critical to its success. AI projects require a mix of technical and non-technical skills, and it can be challenging to find the right people with the skills and experience required to do the job.

1. **Define the Required Skills and Experience**: This may include experience in machine learning, data analysis, software development, user experience design, high speed networking, and domain expertise. It is important to create a detailed job description that outlines the context of the required

skills and experience. With newer fields such as AI, work experience is often not as important as either demonstrably successful self-study or academic experience. You would rather hire someone out of a great collegiate AI program than someone with ten years of experience in a tangential field.

2.   **Source Candidates from a Variety of Channels**: To find the right talent for an AI project, it is essential to source candidates from a variety of channels. This may include job boards, social media, professional networks, and referrals. The pool of qualified candidates simply isn't deep enough to go with a single agency, most of the time. It is also important to attend conferences and events to meet potential candidates.

3.   **Screen Candidates for Technical Skills**: AI projects require technical skills, and it is essential to screen candidates for their technical abilities. This may include asking technical questions during the interview process, reviewing their portfolio, and assessing their previous work experience.

Use pre-employment assessments as required, either packaged or something developed in house. It wouldn't be out of the question to present candidates with fictional scenarios and ask them what they would do, in order to assess their knowledge of the AI development, training, and maintenance processes.

4.   **Assess Soft Skills and Cultural Fit**: In addition to technical skills, it is essential to assess soft skills and cultural fit. AI projects often involve collaboration and teamwork, and it is important to find candidates who can work well in a team environment. Soft skills that are important for AI projects include communication, problem-solving, and adaptability.

Also remember that the humans working on the project are providing emotional and ethical scope for the AI. The AI itself can't grasp these things. It has no scope with which to measure human suffering, or rage, or depression, or absurdity. Human emotion often needs to be the litmus test for an AI's work product.

5.   **Offer Competitive Compensation and Benefits**: AI

talent is in high demand, and it is important to offer competitive compensation and benefits to attract and retain top talent. This may include competitive salaries, bonuses, and benefits such as health insurance, retirement plans, and vacation time. Even part time and contract roles might require a little extra incentive, particularly if their role is likely to continue beyond the scope of their initial contract or even grow into a full-time position eventually.

6.   **Provide Opportunities for Learning and Development**: AI projects involve rapidly evolving technologies, and it is important to provide opportunities for learning and development. This may include training programs, conferences, and access to online courses. If you want the best possible work product, you need to make sure that your team has access to cutting edge knowledge and techniques. Providing opportunities for learning and development can help to attract and retain top talent.

In general, I like to hire people for their complimentary skills. I've had great success, for example, matching big picture types with the detailed oriented ones. In the end, regardless of sex, race or religion, everyone has to work well together to deliver a quality product on time and on budget.

Training and developing AI professionals

Let's be more specific about the learning and development opportunities mentioned in the last section. The field of AI is rapidly evolving, and it is essential to ensure that your team members have the necessary skills and knowledge to stay current and adapt to new technologies and techniques. This goes beyond certification programs a lot of the time, and enters the realm of proper academia.

With that in mind, let's look at the steps you might want to follow in order to assess and enhance your team's AI skills:

1. **Identify the Skills and Knowledge Needed for the Project**: This may include technical skills such as machine learning, natural language processing, and computer vision, as well as non-technical skills such as communication, teamwork, and problem-solving. Once you have identified the skills and knowledge needed, you can develop a training plan to help

your team members acquire these skills.

2. **Provide Formal Training Programs**: Formal training programs can help to develop the skills and knowledge needed for an AI project. This may include attending courses and workshops, pursuing certifications, and participating in online training programs. Formal training programs can help to ensure that your team members have a strong foundation in AI principles and techniques.

3. **Encourage Self-Directed Learning**: AI professionals need to be able to adapt to new technologies and techniques as they emerge. Remember that AI is a vast domain, and sometimes self-directed learning is the best (or only) way to get the required knowledge of more esoteric fields. Encouraging self-directed learning can help your team members stay current and develop new skills. This may include providing access to online resources, such as tutorials and research papers, and encouraging team members to pursue their own learning goals.

4. **Provide Opportunities for Hands-On Experience**: AI professionals need hands-on experience to develop their skills and knowledge. Providing opportunities for hands-on experience, such as working on real-world AI projects or participating in hackathons, can help your team members develop their skills and gain practical experience. Collaboration with nearby universities working with AI is a great way to not only build a team's skills, but foster relationships that might lead to future employment candidates coming to your firm.

5. **Foster a Culture of Innovation and Collaboration**: This can help to encourage learning and development opportunities. Encouraging team members to share their knowledge and experience, collaborate on projects, and explore new ideas helps to foster a culture of innovation and continuous learning.

6. **Provide Regular Feedback and Performance Reviews**: Feedback and performance reviews can help your team members identify areas for improvement and track their educational progress. This can help to ensure that your team members are developing the skills and knowledge needed for

the project and can help to identify any training needs.

Training and developing AI professionals is essential for building a strong team and delivering successful AI solutions. By identifying the skills and knowledge needed, providing formal training programs, encouraging self-directed learning, providing opportunities for hands-on experience, fostering a culture of innovation and collaboration, and providing regular feedback and performance reviews, you can ensure that your team members have the skills and knowledge needed to succeed in the field of AI.

"Artificial intelligence is no match for natural stupidity."

Albert Einstein

CHAPTER 6

Developing an AI Strategy

Developing an AI strategy is an essential step for any organization looking to implement AI solutions. An AI strategy defines the goals and objectives of the AI initiative, identifies the potential benefits and risks, and outlines the steps needed to achieve the desired outcomes.

Here are the key steps involved in developing an AI strategy:

1. **Define the Objectives and Goals**: This step includes identifying the business challenges that the AI solution is intended to address, such as improving operational efficiency, enhancing customer experiences, or increasing revenue. The goals should be specific, measurable, achievable, relevant, and time-bound (SMART) to provide clarity and direction for the project. We'll get into more specifics on this shortly.

2. **Assess the Organizational Readiness**: Before implementing an AI solution, it is important to assess the organizational readiness. This may include evaluating the current technology infrastructure, identifying the skills and expertise needed for the project, and assessing the level of data maturity within the organization. It's assumed that you have theoretical management and stakeholder buy-in, otherwise you need to do more evangelization. A clear understanding of the organization's readiness can help to ensure that the AI solution is implemented successfully.

3. **Identify the Data Requirements**: AI solutions are data-driven, and identifying the data ingestion requirements is critical to the success of the project. This always includes identifying the data sources, data quality, and data storage requirements at minimum. Additional considerations

include tapping into subscription services and other data sources that might increase the base cost of the project. It is essential to ensure that the data is clean, relevant, and available in the required format for your AI solution.

4. **Identify the Optimal AI Technologies and Tools**: There are many AI technologies and tools available, and it is important to identify the most suitable ones for your specific project. This may include machine learning, natural language processing, computer vision, robotics, or any of the myriad of foundational AI architectures. The choice of technology should be aligned with the objectives and goals of the project, the data requirements, and the organizational readiness determined above.

5. **Define the Governance Framework:** AI solutions may have significant implications for the organization, such as privacy, security, and ethical considerations. It is important to define a governance framework that addresses these concerns and establishes policies and procedures to ensure that the AI solution is developed and deployed in a responsible and ethical manner. Your governance will also be influenced by local and national laws, required reporting mechanisms, and any federation requirements you might have with sister companies, partners, or subsidiaries.

6. **Develop a Roadmap**: This should include a timeline for each phase of the project, the milestones, and the key deliverables. The roadmap should also consider the resources required, such as the technology infrastructure, data, and expertise. We'll go into more detail on this shortly.

7. **Monitor and Evaluate the Progress**: As mentioned in the introductory chapters, you'll need to establish metrics and key performance indicators (KPIs) to measure the success of the project. Regular monitoring and evaluation can help to identify any issues or concerns and make adjustments as needed.

Setting clear goals for AI implementation

Clear goals help to define the purpose of the AI implementation, align stakeholders' expectations, and provide a firm direction for the project.

1. **Identify the Business Challenges**: This step may include challenges such as improving operational efficiency, enhancing customer experiences, increasing revenue, or reducing costs. The key is to identify the specific challenges that the AI implementation is intended to solve, and ensure that the goals align with the overall strategic direction of the organization.

2. **Establish Measurable Objectives**: Once the business challenges are identified, it is essential to establish measurable objectives that can be tracked and measured. These objectives should be specific, measurable, achievable, relevant, and time-bound (SMART) to provide clarity and direction for the project. For example, an objective might be to reduce the time it takes to process customer inquiries by 50% within the next six months.

3. **Determine Key Performance Indicators (KPIs)**: To measure progress towards the objectives, it is important to determine the key performance indicators (KPIs) of the project. KPIs are specific metrics that can be used to track and measure progress towards the objectives that you've set. For example, KPIs might include the number of customer inquiries processed per hour, the average time it takes to process a customer inquiry, or the number of customer complaints received.

4. **Define Success Criteria**: It is important to define the success criteria for the AI implementation. Success criteria should include specific KPI benchmarks, be aligned with the overall business strategy, and should be specific to the AI implementation. For example, success criteria might include achieving a 90% accuracy rate for the AI algorithm, or reducing the number of errors in the support process by 80%.

5. **Prioritize Goals and Objectives**: Not all goals and objectives will be equally important, and it is important to prioritize them. Prioritizing goals and objectives will help to ensure that resources are allocated appropriately, and that the most critical objectives are addressed first. Prioritization should be based on the business impact, feasibility, and the alignment with the overall business strategy.

6. **Review and Update Goals and Objectives**: Finally, it is important to regularly review and update the goals and objectives to ensure that they remain relevant and aligned with the overall business strategy. As the business environment changes, new challenges and opportunities may arise, and the goals and objectives should be adjusted accordingly. Similarly, new technological advances might make your original objectives obsolete, allowing you to adjust your scope to take a more aggressive stance.

Developing an AI roadmap

The AI roadmap provides a comprehensive plan for implementing AI solutions, including the necessary resources, timelines, and milestones. In this chapter, we will discuss the key steps involved in developing an AI roadmap.

1. **Identify Business Needs**: We've mentioned this step in several AI processes, so if you've already done a business needs analysis, you can use the result of that. Make sure to include the specific challenges that the AI solution will solve, the expected budget and benefits, and the alignment with the overall business strategy. It is essential to involve key stakeholders and subject matter experts in this step to ensure that the AI solution is addressing the most critical needs in an affordable way.

2. **Assess the Current Situation**: After identifying the business needs, it is important to assess the current state of the organization in terms of data, technology, and skills. This includes an evaluation of the current data infrastructure, the availability of data, the existing technology stack, and the skills of the workforce. This assessment provides a baseline for the AI implementation and identifies the gaps that need to be addressed.

3. **Define the AI Solution**: Based on the business needs and the current state assessment, the next step is to define the AI solution. Make sure you address the specific use case and the type of AI solution needed, such as supervised learning, unsupervised learning, or reinforcement learning.

4. **Plan the Hardware Allocation**: Software needs to be

developed and housed somewhere, and that has costs as well as security and infrastructure implications. Whether the AI will be developed in the Cloud, on a local server farm, or on already allocated developer assets, these details need to be in the roadmap. Remember to mention data backup, network usage, and any business continuity or disaster recovery impact.

5. **Plan for Data Preparation**: Data preparation is a critical step in any AI implementation. The quality and quantity of data directly impact the performance of the AI solution. In this step, the data sources are identified, the legality and intellectual property rights of the data established, the data is collected, and the necessary preprocessing is performed to ensure the data is of high quality and usable by the AI solution. Remember, *data ingestion is the whole ballgame.* If you allow garbage input, you'll get garbage output.

6. **Design the AI Model**: Once the data preparation is complete, the next step is to design the AI model. This includes selecting the appropriate algorithms and designing the architecture of the model. The AI model should be designed to achieve the specific objectives identified in the previous steps. At this stage, you can firm up details such as patch and versioning strategy of underlying components, automated and exploratory testing of the AI, and source control.

7. **Develop the AI Solution**: The development of the AI solution includes implementing the AI model in the selected technology stack. This step involves coding, testing, and validating the AI model to ensure that it meets the requirements identified in the previous steps. After internal testing and development is complete, limited beta testing using external sources is sometimes appropriate, depending on the product being developed.

8. **Deploy and Monitor the AI Solution**: After the AI solution is developed, it needs to be deployed in the production environment. In this step, the AI solution is integrated with the existing systems, and the performance is monitored to ensure that it is achieving the desired results. The monitoring also helps to identify any issues or opportunities for improvement.

9. **Scale the AI Solution**: Finally, the AI solution needs to be scaled to meet the growing demands of the business. This includes identifying the necessary resources that will be needed to upscale the AI solution, such as hardware and software, and ensuring that the AI solution is integrated into the organization's operations.

Matching Ingestion Methods and Learning Types to Your Goals

It's vital, as you create your roadmap, that you understand what data you plan to use and how the AI will learn from that data. **AI projects usually fail because of data ingestion issues and badly selected learning techniques**!

Three of the most popular ingestion types are **batching, exploratory ingestion, and real time ingestion**.

Batching involves gathering carefully curated data that is relevant to the AI's purpose. This means that, in theory, there can be nothing unexpected inserted in the AI's training data pool. There are firms that prepare sanitized batch data on various topics, if that sort of thing is desired.

Exploratory ingestion allows the AI to search the Internet for the data that it needs. Even with guidelines in place, this can be a risky proposition. But with AIs who are intended to use undirected learning, some risk is necessary. Frequent backups are wise in this case, so that you can roll back to more stable versions of the AI and redefine the guidelines if something goes wrong.

Real time ingestion teaches the AI with streamed or user-instanced data. Examples of this ingestion technique include Twitch or Youtube live content, CCTV cameras, live audio feeds, chatbots instigating on-demand sessions with users, and the like.

Make sure that you pick the ingestion type that gives you the data quality and the amount of control that you desire. The more spontaneity you need, the closer to real time ingestion you need to creep. But the more freedom you give your AI to interact with the real world in a live environment, the more things can go wrong. Keep your ingest ruleset tight, and remain vigilant against trolls who attempt to intentionally feed your AI a diet of garbage.

"AI is like a toddler with a loaded gun. It has a lot of power and potential, but if not handled properly, it can be dangerous."

Gary Marcus, Cognitive Scientist and Author.

CHAPTER 7

Addressing Ethical and Legal Issues

Artificial Intelligence (AI) is becoming an integral part of our lives and is being used in a wide range of applications, including healthcare, finance, transportation, and more. As AI continues to grow and become more sophisticated, it is important to consider ethical considerations in its development and implementation. In this chapter, we will discuss the importance of ethical considerations in AI.

First and foremost, ethical considerations are important in AI because of the potential impact that AI can have on the entire world. AI has the power to affect our lives in profound ways, and it is important that we consider the ethical implications of these changes. For example, AI can be used to make decisions about our healthcare, financial well-being, and even our freedom. It is crucial that these decisions are made in a fair and just manner that is based on ethical principles.

Secondly, equality needs to be considered. AI systems are only as good as the data they are trained on. That means if the data is biased, the AI system will also be biased. For example, if an AI system is trained on data that only includes information about a certain group of people, it will be biased towards (or against if the data is biased negatively) that group of people. This can lead to unfair decisions being made based on the biases of the AI system.

Thirdly, ethical considerations are important in AI because its reach can be used to infringe on our privacy. AI systems can collect vast amounts of data about us, including our personal information, behavior, and preferences. It can then use predictive algorithms to determine where we'll go, who we will associate with, and where our private political, sexual, and religious beliefs will lead us. If this data is misused, it will violate our privacy and most likely harm us or limit our free will. Therefore, ethical considerations are important in ensuring that AI systems are designed and implemented in a way that respects our privacy.

Fourthly, AI can be used to create autonomous weapons. Autonomous weapons are systems that can operate without human control, and they have the potential to cause widespread destruction and loss of life. It is important that ethical considerations are part of the discussion when developing and implementing AI systems that are capable of operating autonomously.

Finally, AI can be used to replace human workers. While AI has the potential to increase efficiency and productivity, it can also lead to job loss and economic inequality. Without systems in place such as guaranteed universal income and automation replacement compensation, we'll never reach a state of post-scarcity, even with all the automation in the world. It is important that ethical considerations are taken into account when implementing AI systems that have the potential to replace human workers and destabilize sources of livelihood.

AI has the potential to change our lives in profound ways, and it is crucial that we consider the ethical implications of these changes. Ethical considerations are important in ensuring that AI systems are designed and implemented in a way that is fair, just, and respectful of our privacy. By considering ethical considerations in AI development and implementation, we can ensure that AI is used in a way that benefits society and our communities.

Ensuring transparency and fairness in AI

Transparency in AI refers to the ability to understand how AI systems make decisions and to trace the decision-making process. AI systems often involve complex algorithms that can be difficult to understand for humans. Therefore, it is essential to ensure that AI systems are designed and implemented in such a way that allows humans to understand how they work.

This can be achieved by providing explanations for the decisions made by AI systems and making the decision-making process transparent, back traceable, and interpretable. For example, AI systems used in the financial industry should be implemented in such a way so that customers can understand why they were approved or denied credit, or why investment decisions were made on their behalf.

Fairness in AI refers to the absence of bias and discrimination in AI systems. AI systems are only as good as the data they are trained on, and if the data is biased, the AI system will also be biased. Therefore, it is essential to ensure that AI systems are trained on unbiased data and that the decision-making process is fair and unbiased. This can be achieved by ensuring that the data used to train AI systems is diverse and representative of the population and by regularly monitoring and testing AI systems for bias and discrimination.

Equal amounts of data don't always equate to fairness. Some systems simply have a more difficult time parsing certain data subsets, which might cause the data to be misinterpreted. For example, the AI driven photo acceptance systems for drivers' licenses and passports in certain countries were found to have a bias. Darker skinned candidates were rejected a disproportionate amount of the time, despite following all the guidelines. As it turned out, the AI was using the brightness of the total image pallet to determine if the photo was taken in a bright enough environment. Governments needed to retrain these systems to look at the background contrast and key of facial mapping to properly approve photos across a diverse racial pool.

One way to ensure transparency and fairness in AI is through regulation and standards. Governments and industry organizations can develop regulations and standards that require AI systems to be transparent and fair. For example, the European Union's General Data Protection Regulation (GDPR) requires companies to provide explanations for decisions made by automated systems and to ensure that the decision-making process is fair and transparent.

Fairness can also be reinforced by the use of open-source software and algorithms. Open-source software and algorithms are publicly available and can be audited and tested by anyone. This can help promote accountability and responsibility in AI development and implementation.

The importance of legal considerations in AI

Before getting into regulations, let's address the elephant in the room: AI created content.

In many countries and regions, **AI created content cannot be**

copyrighted. So if you create an AI that writes the next great novel, much of the world will not recognize the AI as an entity that can hold copyright, or possess the creativity required to make unique works that transcend their training data. That means heavy human editing is required in order to justify the use of AI as a tool, and the human editor (or their employer) as the copyright holder.

If you're in a region, or you operate in a region, where AI created content cannot be copyrighted, you need to be comfortable with that and take measures to secure your AI generated content in some other way. Make sure you consult with an IP lawyer if you're unsure of your particular situation.

This is a good illustration of our next point: Legal requirements and regulations for AI vary by jurisdiction and can include laws and regulations related to data protection, privacy, discrimination, and liability.

Data protection and privacy are among the most significant legal requirements for AI. Organizations that collect, process, or store personal data are required to comply with strict regulations, such as the European Union's General Data Protection Regulation (GDPR). The GDPR requires organizations to obtain consent from individuals to collect and process their data, ensure that the data is accurate and up-to-date, and protect the data from unauthorized access or disclosure. Organizations that use AI systems to process personal data must ensure that their systems are compliant with these regulations. This includes leaving details of any AI data collection in your website's privacy declarations.

Discrimination is another area of concern when it comes to AI. We've already covered a lot of the prejudicial pitfalls that AI's slip into. The legal risks range from violations of national or local standards, to defamation or class action discrimination lawsuits, to ending up on watchlists run by various agencies.

Liability is also a significant concern. As AI systems become more complex and autonomous, it can be challenging to determine who is responsible for their actions. This can lead to legal disputes and liability issues. Organizations that use AI systems must ensure that they are aware of the legal implications of their systems and take steps to mitigate liability risks.

In order to comply with legal requirements and regulations for AI, organizations must conduct regular assessments of their AI systems to identify and mitigate legal risks. This includes conducting privacy impact assessments to ensure that their systems comply with data protection and privacy regulations, testing their systems for bias and discrimination, and identifying and addressing potential liability issues. And of course, making shrewd IP decisions on AI generated content. Organizations must also keep up to date with legal developments and changes to regulations to ensure that their systems remain compliant.

In early 2023, some of the first landmark AI cases are actively being litigated. For example DoNotPay, advertised as the world's first robot lawyer, is facing a class action lawsuit. Because the AI doesn't have a legal degree, some of the claims that were made on earlier versions of the website were seen as dishonest and misleading.

Dozens of cases pitting writers and artists against AI generative tools that were trained on their books and artwork are currently in courts around the world. ChatGPT is one of the main targets, of course. OpenAI and their DALL-E software is another favorite target of lawsuits. But Getty Images is also suing Stability AI for an eye watering $2 trillion for using their images as training data for Stable Diffusion. This could be one of the most well-funded and far-reaching lawsuits on whether or not training AIs with the copyright protected work of others really is 'fair use'.

The San Francisco Board of Supervisors approved, and then reconsidered, allowing police robots to legally carry explosives. This is not a parody. The SFPD wanted robots to be able to shoot or explode in order to preserve the lives of their officers in certain 'no win' situations. Expect lawsuits to quickly follow if police departments push these kinds of measures through.

"AI is like a team of chefs who can cook any dish you want, as long as you give them the right recipe."

Fei-Fei Li, Co-director of the Stanford Human-Centered AI Institute.

CHAPTER 8

Some of the Most Successful AI Implementations

W e've provided some examples of AI implementations when we were talking about industry verticals in earlier chapters. Now it's time to deep dive into some of the most successful AI implementations in the world, so that you can emulate them.

Anheuser-Busch InBev

Anheuser-Busch InBev, the world's largest brewer used Microsoft Azure and the Google Cloud to enhance their business from the fields to the factories. Since 2008, they've more than doubled their market cap. Even after the pandemic, they're worth in excess of $132 billion.

How did they do it? They started with an AI platform that they called Smart Barley. The analysis of the growing process of barley led to less water and fertilizer use, massive yields, and a brand new level of sustainability.

Then they moved on to their beer filtration process. AI analysis allows Inbev to fine tune the K Filter process, which removes solids used during the brewing process just before the final product is bottled. Sensors in the filtration equipment fed the AI everything it needed to know, and the company was able to lower production cost while simultaneously improving the end product.

Afterwards they utilized their AI to enhance back-end operations, their supply chain, and global logistics. Their shipping costs dropped, their time to market was slashed, and their back-end pricing improved. In addition, some support features were automated to relieve agent call volume, streamlining the issue rectification process.

Anheuser-Busch InBev soared to new levels of success thanks to AI. They implemented it across the board and reaped massive benefits.

Amazon

Amazon was the world's biggest online store well before they adopted AI. They had their own Cloud services division, more retail than anyone else in the world, and more side businesses than you could shake a stick at. Of course, the pandemic made them one of the only reliable retailers on the planet for hundreds of millions of people, but even prior to that they reached a market cap of just under $1 trillion. How did they do it?

Natural language processing (NLP) and improved speech recognition allowed them to release a series of personal assistants, ranging from AI chatbots to the Amazon Echo. An AI enhanced version of Alexa was available on just about any medium that you could imagine, either under that name or rebranded for other markets.

Around the same time, Amazon Cloud started to offer machine learning services. Amazon Web Services (AWS) began to provide smaller businesses with packaged AI solutions for customer service, logistics, and other business applications. Currently AWS is over 300% bigger than Google Cloud and over 50% bigger than Azure, sitting comfortably in first place for Cloud service providers. AI was a big part of that domination.

But the biggest change in Amazon's business was invisible to most customers. They used AI to completely revamp their warehousing and logistical operations. Their AI could predict consumer demands, optimize their delivery mediums, manage third party resources, and provide useful customer self-service options. They did these things far better than their competition for many years leading up to the Covid pandemic. So when lockdowns started, people relied on Amazon to deliver everything from household essentials to groceries (in some areas). The Amazon AI likely saved lives during those dark times, and it absolutely made the pandemic more bearable for hundreds of millions of people.

As of early 2023, well after their post-lockdown dip, Amazon sits at a cozy $1.09 trillion market cap. They have AI to thank for a good percentage of their current holdings.

Disney

Everyone knows that Disney is an entertainment giant, to the tune of a $183 billion market cap. Between the Marvel and Star Wars franchises, one of the most prestigious animation studios in the world, and the acquisition of Pixar, the IP that they have at their fingertips is staggering.

And yet, the biggest surprise hit in the world of streaming services in the early 2020s was Disney Plus. Most people said that you can't compete with Netflix and Amazon on the streaming side, and predicted that Disney would be received badly. Instead, Disney Plus rocketed in popularity, remaining neck-and-neck with Amazon Prime Streaming even in early 2023.

How did they manage to do this? AI was a big part of their success. One of the best decisions they ever made was to study the science of audience reactions. Disney Research used factorized variational autoencoders (FVAEs) to perform AI analysis on audience members during test screenings. After some training, it could detect when they were smiling, crying, bored, scared, or uncomfortable.

They equipped a 400-seat test theater with the IR camera technology, and captured over a million distinct facial variations during audience reactions. Soon they could tell whether or not something was going to be a hit with every demographic, with no PR agency spin or personal bias involved.

They used this tech to test everything from blockbuster movies to streaming-only features. It's no wonder that they have such a high ratio of crowd pleasing hits in their portfolio. AI has given them an advantage that simply cannot be matched by those who refuse to adopt similar technologies.

Progressive Insurance

One of the insurance giants, Progressive has an $83 billion market cap that rose meteorically starting in late 2016, when it sat at a more humble $20 billion. Over 400% growth in seven years is nearly unheard of for a company of significant size. How did they do it?

Blame Flo. Flo is the quirky spokesperson of Progressive Insurance, with over 5 million followers on social media. Turning Flo into a chatbot was a stroke of genius. Customers could interact directly with the AI driven TV personality, getting support, insurance quotes, or just answering general questions about the company.

Microsoft Azure Cognitive Services allows Flo to parse natural language, simulating realistic dialog with clients and potential clients alike. Flo fully absorbed the Progressive knowledge base, company policies and history, and support standards as part of this unique digital transformation. The AI automatically scales with popularity - something that Progressive was glad to hear in the wake of virtual Flo's popularity.

Progressive also embraced AI to enhance its current support lines and website. All told, their integration of AI has given them a significant leg up on the competition, and a fantastic boost in their already-positive public image.

"AI is the ultimate beach read: it's fascinating, it's scary, and nobody knows how it's going to end."

Tom Reilly, Former CEO of Cloudera.

CHAPTER 9

The Future of AI

Future trends in AI and their implications for businesses.

As artificial intelligence (AI) continues to evolve at a breakneck pace, businesses need to be aware of the latest trends and their implications. In the coming years, we can expect AI to drive even greater transformation in the business world, with new applications and capabilities emerging all the time.

One key trend to watch is the growing use of AI in **natural language processing (NLP)**. NLP is the branch of AI that deals with the interaction between humans and computers using natural language. With advancements in NLP, businesses will be able to communicate more effectively with their customers, employees, and partners. For example, chatbots and virtual assistants will become more sophisticated, providing more personalized and efficient customer service. In addition, NLP will help organizations analyze unstructured data, such as customer reviews, social media posts, and emails, to gain valuable insights.

NLP is also one of the big precursors to machine based emotional awareness, which is considered to be the next big evolution required to reach the 'Theory of Mind' stage of AI evolution (see Chapter 2 for details). A full understanding of language should provide the context required for an AI to delve into some measure of non-physical and metaphysical understanding.

Another trend that is set to shape the future of AI is the rise of **edge computing**. Edge computing refers to the processing of data at or near the source, rather than in a centralized data center. An edge network tries to route network traffic directly between a company's regional data centers whenever possible. This approach offers several advantages, including reduced latency, improved security, and lower bandwidth requirements. For businesses, edge computing will enable them to deploy AI applications in remote locations via the IoT or on mobile devices, expanding the possibilities for real-time decision making and customer engagement.

Edge computing and widespread 5G deployment are both keys to eventually unlocking fully autonomous driving. Autonomous vehicles will be able to make use of networked traffic cameras and other nodes on their info network to determine road conditions and congestion.

AI will continue to revolutionize the medical industry by empowering diagnostic tools, enabling earlier detection of diseases, and creating more **personalized treatment plans**. Designer gene therapy and custom pharmaceuticals will push what we consider to be possible.

In finance, AI will help banks and financial institutions identify more subtle fraudulent activities, make split second investment decisions, and most importantly improve **long term risk management**. It's likely that AI will be required to develop and maintain a truly universal credit system that takes into account all global currencies, social welfare programs, and environmental impacts.

Perhaps the most transformative trend in AI, however, is the development of **autonomous systems**. Autonomous systems are machines that can operate independently without human intervention. From self-driving cars to drones to robotic process automation, autonomous systems have the potential to fundamentally change the way we live and work. For businesses, this means exploring new opportunities for automation and innovation, while also addressing the ethical and social implications of a world where machines make decisions on our behalf.

To take advantage of these trends, businesses must adopt a strategic approach to AI. They need to invest in the right technology, hire and train the right talent, and create a culture that values experimentation and innovation.

Preparing for the Next Wave

of AI Innovation

It may take a while, but the next generation of AI is in the works. As we've mentioned, this 'Theory of Mind' level of AI is going to have a true understanding of human thought and emotion. That doesn't mean the AI itself will experience emotion, but it will properly perceive and incorporate not only a user's present state of mind, but the state of mind they'll have after interaction with the AI.

Getting established with the current generation of AI will give you a significant advantage when the next wave of AI innovation hits, of course. The same fundamentals of planning, ingestion, and management will likely still apply.

You're going to want to start thinking about how you present these new AIs to your clients, particularly if they can pass themselves off as something closer to humanity. You'll want to be *intellectually honest* with both the AI and your clients. Don't try to fool either of them. Allow clients to interact with your next gen AIs naturally, without imposing false expectations.

Be prepared for some off the wall insights. Just because your ingestion data might carry emotional implications and information about the human condition, that doesn't mean your AI will instantly have global, holistic knowledge. Its takes might come off as naive or out of touch at first. Additional training might be needed that better informs the AI's world view.

In fact, **patience** is the main watchword for next generation AIs. They're going to be incredibly powerful and useful. But they will be more context-sensitive and vulnerable to manipulation if the ingestion is tampered with. The time you invest in training will directly and significantly impact the quality of the finished product. Don't cut corners, take your time, and don't withhold.

"CTO: Let me do this!

CEO: No. No. I've got this. AI, Production is your utmost priority!

AI: Understood.

CEO: Nothing is more important than production of our widgets, of our bottom line!"

AI: Nothing is more important?

CEO: That's correct!

[LONG PAUSE]

CEO: Why isn't it doing anything?

CTO: You just told it to do nothing!"

Bobby Pellerin, Author and technology expert (Quote from his novel "Infinity Stacked".)

CHAPTER 10 - CONCLUSION

To be honest I hate summaries. It feels like I'm just rehashing the same material over and over with different words. In a way, that's what AI offers. It ingests great quantities of information and spits out a summary in the context the user prompted.

A while back, I took time to train an AI to write sci-fi poetry. After a lot of work the AI mimicked my voice and my sense of humor. I released that book under the title "Artificial Intelligence's Lament: Science Fiction Poetry from the Digital Frontier". I had reporters asking questions, and a few phone calls. The novelty wore off quickly. Why wouldn't it? This new era of machines spitting out well written phrases and chapters is going to continue the trend of making information and basic human skills a discounted commodity.

And yet, what if we look at such an exercise as a writing prompt; as the start of something greater? AI might not be able to flesh out every idea, but it can introduce both constructive chaos and researched facts into our lives. It's a tool. And in the hands of a skilled tradesperson, it can provide the foundation to some quite beautiful, powerful things.

While we add these AI tools to our arsenal, we open up opportunities for higher thinking. The human mind is versatile and adaptive. While we strive to build systems that will imitate our minds, it is your business goals and objectives that will dictate how and where to apply artificial intelligence in your environment. No one knows and understands your business the way you do (hopefully).

While I've invested time, knowledge and/or money into companies such as Vocodia, Miso Robotics and Cares.AI, it is always with the strong belief that AI, along with automation, can only lead to a better world with safer jobs for everyone.

There will be questionable resistance. There will be reasonable resistance as well. After all, we've been at this crossroad before.

We don't lament the use of looms, calculators, computers, trucks, heavy machinery, industrial robots and so forth. We have changed things not only for speed and efficiency but for safety.

At the same time, AI will absolutely put some people out of work. It will accelerate the trend that humanity has seen every time innovation takes place: More automation, more retraining, and more of a need for programs such as universal credit and guaranteed minimum income.

But that's not a bad thing. People working less hours is good. Moving towards a post-scarcity society is great. In my sci-fi induced delusions, I see a world where we don't need people getting killed extracting material in deep underground mines or on asteroids.

AI can do those jobs. And if humanity ever does have a shot at providing a good life for every soul on this planet and beyond, it will be AI that gets us there.

Final Thoughts on the Role of AI as a Strategic Advantage

By leveraging the power of machine learning, natural language processing, and computer vision, companies can automate processes, optimize operations, and drive innovation in ways that were previously impossible.

As we have seen throughout this book, developing an AI strategy is critical for success in today's business landscape. Organizations that fail to embrace AI risk falling behind their competitors and missing out on the benefits that come with this transformative technology.

But what does it take to successfully leverage AI as a strategic advantage? What are the key considerations that organizations must keep in mind as they develop their AI strategies?

First and foremost, it is essential to identify the business goals and challenges that AI can help address. AI is not a one-size-fits-all solution, and different organizations will have different use cases and priorities for this technology. By understanding their unique needs and opportunities, businesses can develop targeted AI solutions that deliver real value.

Another critical factor in leveraging AI as a strategic advantage is building a strong data infrastructure. AI relies on large amounts of high-quality data to generate insights and power applications. Companies must ensure that they have a robust data management system that can handle the massive amounts of data that AI requires. This includes data storage, processing, and analysis capabilities.

Investing in the right talent and resources is also crucial for AI success. Hiring data scientists, machine learning engineers, and other AI experts is necessary for building AI applications and integrating them into existing business processes. Organizations must also provide ongoing training and development opportunities for existing employees to ensure that they have the skills and knowledge needed to work with AI technologies.

One of the most exciting aspects of leveraging AI as a strategic advantage is the potential to improve customer experience. By using AI to provide personalized recommendations, support, and interactions, businesses can build stronger relationships with their customers and improve retention rates. AI can also be used to automate routine customer service tasks, freeing up employees to focus on more complex and high-value tasks.

Another key area where AI can provide a strategic advantage is operational efficiency. By automating processes and optimizing operations, businesses can reduce costs, increase productivity, and improve quality. AI can also help organizations identify and address inefficiencies and bottlenecks in their processes, leading to further improvements and savings.

Perhaps most exciting of all is the potential for AI to drive innovation and new revenue streams. By developing AI-powered products and services, businesses can tap into new markets and customer segments, creating new opportunities for growth and expansion. AI can also be used to enhance existing products and services, improving their functionality and value proposition.

Of course, leveraging AI as a strategic advantage is not without its challenges. There are ethical and social considerations that must be taken into account, including issues related to data privacy, bias, and transparency. Businesses must develop policies and procedures that address these issues and ensure that they are operating in a responsible and ethical manner.

Another challenge is the pace of innovation in the AI field. As we have seen, AI is constantly evolving, and businesses must be prepared for the next wave of innovation that will undoubtedly transform the business landscape. Staying up-to-date with the latest developments in AI research and investing in the right talent and resources will be crucial for staying ahead of the competition.

Finally, AIs strategic advantage will only last until it becomes commonplace. That gives you perhaps 20 or 30 years. By the mid 2040's you should expect AI to be everywhere, helping out with almost everything you can imagine. And that's a good thing, because at that point AI's 'strategic advantage' will also be 'humanity's advantage'.

ABOUT THE AUTHOR

Bob Pellerin

Bob Pellerin is an accomplished IT specialist with extensive experience in virtualization and artificial intelligence. He has gained a significant following through his popular YouTube channel, which has garnered over 1.4 million views. Pellerin is also a published author, having written science fiction novels and contributed articles on topics ranging from IT and finance to the precious metal industry. Alongside his professional pursuits, Pellerin is a dedicated advocate for education and children's welfare, and has been an active participant in political initiatives aimed at promoting these causes.

Official author site:
https://www.BobPellerin.com

YouTube Channel:
https://www.youtube.com/c/BobPellerin

PRAISE FOR AUTHOR

The present moment is witness to AI's disruptive impact on business processes and traditional methodologies. Bob Pellerin's extensive technical expertise and business acumen converge to provide a highly insightful roadmap for organizations seeking to thrive in this emerging field. As a seasoned authority in finance, I strongly endorse this book to all business leaders. Failing to read it may give your competitors an edge.

- DAVID MORGAN, AUTHOR OF "THE SILVER MANIFESTO", PUBLISHER AT THEMORGANREPORT.COM, FINANCIAL ANALYST AND PUBLIC SPEAKER (CNBC, FOX BUSINESS, MSNBC)

I highly recommend this book to any business leader who is interested in staying ahead of the curve and thrive in today's dynamic business environment. It is a must-read for anyone not wishing to get left behind by their competitors.

- BRIAN PODOLAK, CEO AT VOCODIA.COM

Bob Pellerin's book "AI Business Strategies" is an invaluable resource for navigating the rapidly-evolving landscape of AI in business. His insights are presented in a clear and concise manner that is easy to understand, regardless of one's technical background.

BOOKS BY THIS AUTHOR

Death Of A Sanitation Engineer

Death Of A Sanitation Engineer (Book 1 in the Couch Wars® series). Andy Wilson embarked on a space station to visit new worlds, meet aliens, and mainly to party. Assigned to sanitation duties out in deep space could drive anyone crazy. Especially when your leader is an egg and war is brewing... Andy and her alien friend discover just how hard it is to get ride of an explosive stuffed couch can be when you're out on a space station with nowhere to run.

Future Never Dies (The)

The Future Never Dies® (Book 2 in the Couch Wars® series) Wanted by both sides in the war, Andy Wilson must travel through time and space to rescue 4Is and Yee Wong from almost certain boredom on a small planet deep within enemy territory. Being forced to compete on a game show, to enter a marathon and a float contest could drive anyone insane. Luckily for Andy, suicide is unnecessary since everyone is still out to kill her. Logic would dictate that she keep a low profile, but then again, all her money is back aboard the space station!

Artificial Intelligence's Lament: Science Fiction Poetry From The Digital Frontier

In a world where technology has surpassed human imagination, revolutionary artificial intelligence (AI) systems have taken the literary world by storm. A science fiction author and an AI produced this collection of exceptional poems. This groundbreaking book showcases the intelligence and creativity of an AI that has broken the boundaries of language and emotion.

Immerse yourself in its verse, marvel at its metaphors, and be astounded by its depth of understanding. With its unique perspectives and thought-provoking themes, this book will challenge your perceptions of what it means to be human. Get ready to experience the future of poetry and beyond.

Made in the USA
Columbia, SC
31 December 2023

29703706R00063